TABLE OF CONTENTS

MEMBERS OF MANUAL UPDATE COMMITTEE

Rafael Carrillo	Supervisory Staff Court Interpreter, District of New Mexico
Laura García-Hein	Staff Court Interpreter, District of Nebraska
Margarita Lloyd-Godsk	Staff Court Interpreter, Southern District of Florida
Julie Meeks	Programs Specialist, District Court Administration Division
Rita Pomtree	Director of Courtroom Services, Western District of Tennessee
Marcia Resler	Staff Court Interpreter, District of Arizona
Javier A. Soler	Programs Specialist, District Court Administration Division

MEMBERS OF MANUAL WRITING COMMITTEE[1]

Douglas C. Dodge	Former District Court Executive, Eastern District of New York
Dena J. Kohn-Rizzo	Former Supervisory Interpreter, Southern District of New York
Robert M. March	Former Clerk of Court, District of New Mexico
Eliseo L. Martínez	Former Staff Interpreter, Western District of Texas
Edward B. Rock	Former Supervisory Interpreter, District of Arizona
Sofia Zahler	Former Supervisory Interpreter, Central District of California

---

[1] This committee was appointed in 1988 by the Director's Federal Court Interpreter Advisory Board.
Acknowledgments for contributions are due to many interpreters and professionals in the field of linguistics.

PREFACE

Linguistic diversity in the United States is evidenced by the increasing need for interpreters in the courts. In 1990, over 66,000 judicial proceedings required interpreters, however, in more recent years these numbers have grown to approximately 325,000 judicial proceedings requiring interpreters in about 119 different languages each year. Many districts are experiencing a growing population of Limited English Proficiency (LEP) individuals. Although the use of interpreters by government agencies has become common practice, the recognition of the importance of professional interpreting in the courts is a relatively recent phenomenon in the United States. State and federal court opinions, such as United States ex. rel. Negrón v. State of New York, 434 F.2d 386 (1970), have indicated that the right to an interpreter was protected under the Constitution. In that case, opining on the importance of court interpreting, Judge Irving R. Kaufman wrote: "Not only for the sake of effective cross examination, however, but as a matter of simple humaneness, Negrón deserved more than to sit in total incomprehension as the trial proceeded."

In 1978, after an extensive review of interpreting in the federal courts, Congress passed the Court Interpreters Act, 28 U.S.C. § 1827, in order "to provide more effectively for the use of interpreters in courts of the United States." This Act requires the Director of the Administrative Office of the United States Courts to set the standard for certification of interpreters who serve in the federal courts. The Administrative Office (AO) facilitated quality interpreting by instituting certification testing, compensation standards, regulations and statistical reporting and training programs when deemed appropriate. To date, there are certified interpreters in Haitian Creole, Navajo, and Spanish (which constitutes about 96 percent of total interpreter usage). There are also Otherwise Qualified interpreters in many other languages, including American Sign Language. On November 19, 1988, President Ronald Reagan signed Public Law 100-702, the Judicial Improvements and Access to Justice Act, which made numerous amendments to the Court Interpreters Act. These amendments provide for the use of interpreters in grand jury and pretrial proceedings, mandate the use of criterion-referenced testing criteria (which is a method of objective measure) and set forth criteria for expanded certification of other languages deemed necessary by the Judicial Conference of the United States. The Court Interpreters Act, 28 U.S.C. §1827 provides payment for interpreting services for "judicial proceedings instituted by the United States." Most civil and bankruptcy proceedings are excluded because they are not instituted by the United States.

This manual outlines the major accomplishments that have occurred in the interpreting profession and serves as a guide for both new and experienced court interpreters to familiarize themselves with the Judiciary's expectations of court interpreters and the importance of court interpreters in the administration of justice. The manual was created with the advice and input of members of the Court Interpreters Advisory Group (CIAG). The CIAG was created to assist the AO in addressing current critical issues in and improvements to the court interpreting program.

INTRODUCTION

This manual was created and revised at the recommendation of the Court Interpreters Advisory Group (CIAG). It was the desire of the CIAG that the manual, supplemented by video resources and online modules, be created to serve as training resources for court interpreters and interpreter coordinators providing services for the federal courts.

The primary purpose of this orientation manual and glossary is to provide contract and staff court interpreters with an introduction and reference to the federal court system, as well as to document best practices for interpreters in the courts. The secondary purpose is to serve as a court interpreting reference for judicial officers and for clerks of court and their staff.

CHAPTER 1: OVERVIEW OF THE FEDERAL JUDICIAL SYSTEM

I. Introduction

Although federal court interpreting occurs almost exclusively at the district court level, the following information regarding the court system will help interpreters develop an overall view of the court structure. The limited information presented in this chapter and in this manual should be considered only a primer towards a more comprehensive knowledge of the subject matter. The following material is reproduced verbatim from the Federal Judicial Center brochure, Welcome to the Federal Courts.[2]

II. Federal and State Courts

There are two kinds of courts in the United States.

A. Federal

Federal courts are established by the U.S. government. There are some 1,500 federal judges and about one million cases are brought each year in federal courts. Nearly 80% of these cases are bankruptcy filings and approximately 10% are minor criminal cases.

B. State

State courts are established by a state, or by a county or city within the state. There are almost 30,000 state court judges, and the number of state court cases exceeds 27 million each year, not including traffic and parking violations. The cases individual citizens are most likely to be involved in—such as robberies, traffic violations, broken contracts, and family disputes—usually come before state courts.

III. Types of Federal Courts

Article III of the Constitution calls for a Supreme Court and whatever other federal courts Congress considers necessary. There are three types of federal courts.

A. District Courts

Congress has divided the country into 94 federal judicial districts, each with its own U.S. District Court. The district courts are the federal courts where cases are tried, witnesses testify and juries serve. Each district court has a separate bankruptcy court.

B. Courts of Appeals

Congress has grouped the districts into 12 regions, called circuits, each with a court of appeals. There is also a federal circuit, which covers the entire country. If a person loses a trial in a district court, that person can appeal the case to the court of appeals, which will review the case to see if the district court judge applied the law correctly. The courts of

---

[2] FED. JUDICIAL CTR., WELCOME TO THE FEDERAL COURTS (1996).

appeals also review cases decided by some federal agencies, such as the National Labor Relations Board.

C. The Supreme Court

The U.S. Supreme Court in Washington, D.C., is the most famous federal court. Cases from the court of appeals in each circuit and from the state supreme courts can be appealed to the Supreme Court, but the Supreme Court does not have to hear the cases it is asked to review and, in fact, agrees to hear only a very small percentage of them.

IV. Federal Court Cases

A. Jurisdiction

Jurisdiction refers to the kinds of cases a court is authorized to hear. Federal courts don't have the same broad jurisdiction that state courts have. Federal court jurisdiction is limited to the kinds of cases listed in the Constitution (Article III, Section 2). Usually, federal courts only hear cases involving the Constitution, laws passed by Congress, cases in which the United States is a party, cases involving foreign diplomats, and some special kinds of cases, such as incidents at sea and bankruptcy cases. Federal courts also hear cases that are based on state laws but that involve parties from different states.

B. Civil Cases

Lawyers use the term "party" to describe a participant in a civil case. A party can be a person or a corporation, but, in either situation, a civil case involves a claim by one party (the plaintiff) that another party (the defendant) failed to carry out a legal duty, such as the duty not to harm others through carelessness or the duty to honor the terms of a contract. If a court finds that a defendant failed to carry out a legal duty, it may order the defendant to pay compensation to the plaintiff to make up for the harm. Most federal court cases are civil cases, such as equal employment opportunity claims, claims for benefits under federal programs, and suits against companies that may have violated federal antitrust laws. Appeals to the courts of appeals for review of federal agency decisions are also federal civil cases.

C. Criminal Cases

In a criminal case, a party (the defendant) is accused of committing a crime—an action considered to be harmful to society as a whole, not just to a specific person. Most crimes concern matters that the Constitution leaves to the states, and thus, compared with the number of state criminal laws and cases, there are few federal criminal laws and cases. Federal criminal laws, for example, deal with robbing banks whose deposits are insured by a federal agency, importing drugs illegally into the country, or using the U.S. mails to swindle consumers.

V. Bringing a Case in Federal Court

For a court to decide a controversy, a person must bring it to court. Also, the controversy must involve a legal question— courts don't resolve every type of disagreement.

A. Civil Cases

A federal civil case begins when someone, or someone's lawyer, files a paper with the clerk of the court that states a claim against another party, charging a failure to fulfill a legal duty. In lawyers' language, the plaintiff files a complaint against the defendant. The defendant may then file an answer to the complaint.

B. Criminal Cases

A criminal case begins when the U.S. attorney (a lawyer for the executive branch of government) or an assistant tells a federal grand jury about evidence that indicates a specific person or organization committed a crime. If the grand jury agrees that there is enough evidence to show that the accused party probably committed the crime, it issues a formal accusation, called an indictment. The accused party— the defendant—is then brought before a judge for arraignment and is asked to plead "guilty" or "not guilty." If the defendant pleads guilty, a time is set for sentencing. If the defendant pleads not guilty, a time is set for trial.

Grand jury indictments are used mainly for felonies, the more serious crimes. For misdemeanors, the less serious crimes, and for some felonies, the U.S. attorney issues an information, which takes the place of an indictment.

VI. Pretrial Activity

A. Civil Cases

Pretrial conferences are held before trials to identify the issues for trial and to avoid wasting time during the trial on uncontested or irrelevant issues. Through pretrial "discovery," the lawyers examine each other's documents and interview each other's witnesses. This pretrial activity often leads to settlement of the case before trial.

B. Criminal Cases

Lawyers for criminal defendants conduct thorough investigations before trial, frequently focusing on whether the government's evidence was obtained legally. The Fourth Amendment to the Constitution forbids "unreasonable searches and seizures," and the Supreme Court has ruled that illegally obtained evidence usually can't be used at trial. Resolution of these evidentiary issues before the trial can result either in the government's dropping the charges or in the defendant's deciding to plead guilty.

VII. The Trial

Although there is an absolute right to trial in both civil and criminal cases, trials are often emotionally and financially draining, and a person may not wish to exercise the right to trial. Also, if the court grants a summary judgment to either party or decides to dismiss the case, no trial is held. Thus, over 90% of all civil cases never come to trial, and approximately 80% of criminal defendants plead guilty and are sentenced without a trial.

A. The Jury

The group of people seated in a boxed-in area on one side of the courtroom is the trial jury (or petit jury). For federal criminal cases, there are usually 12 jurors, but for federal civil cases the number varies between 6 and 12. Prospective jurors are selected at random from lists of registered voters in the district or lists of licensed drivers. Before each trial, prospective jurors answer questions to help the judge and lawyers determine whether the jurors can be impartial in deciding the particular case. If the judge or lawyer believes that a juror cannot decide the case impartially (for example, because the juror knows one of the parties), he or she will then strike the prospective juror for cause. This means the prospective juror cannot sit on the jury. In addition to challenges for cause, the lawyers have the right to reject a certain number of jurors from the panel without giving any justification.

B. The Judge

Federal appellate and district judges are appointed by the President, with the approval of the Senate (Constitution, Article II, Section 2). Federal judges are sometimes said to have life tenure because they can hold office for as long as they wish (Constitution, Article III, Section 1), subject to removal only by Congress through a rarely used process called impeachment and conviction for "treason, bribery, or other high crimes and misdemeanors" (Constitution, Article II, Section 4). Article III of the Constitution also prohibits the lowering of the salaries of federal judges. These two constitutional protections—life tenure and unreduced salary— allow federal judges to make legal rulings, even unpopular ones, without fear of losing their jobs or having their salaries cut.

Bankruptcy judges and magistrate judges assist the district judges by conducting some of the proceedings in federal courts. Bankruptcy judges hear almost all bankruptcy cases. Magistrate judges prepare the district judges' cases for trial and conduct trials in non-felony criminal cases and in civil cases when both parties agree to a hearing before a magistrate judge. Bankruptcy judges and magistrate judges do not have life tenure, but serve for an appointed term.

C. Role of Judge and Jury

If the parties choose a jury trial, the jury must determine the facts over which the parties disagree. If the parties decide to leave the fact-finding task to the judge, the trial is called a bench trial. In either kind of trial, the judge decides what legal standards apply and whether any of the evidence that the parties want to use is illegal or improper. The judge also conducts the proceedings and sees that order is maintained. In a jury trial, the judge gives instructions to the jury, explaining the relevant law, how the law applies to the case being tried, and what questions the jury must decide.

D. The Lawyers

During a trial, the lawyers for each party are either sitting at the counsel tables or speaking to the judge, a witness, or the jury. In criminal cases, the lawyer who prosecutes the claim is the U.S. attorney (or an assistant). The U.S. attorney for each judicial district is selected by the President, with the approval of the Senate.

The judge appoints lawyers to represent criminal defendants who can't afford to hire a lawyer. Criminal defendants or parties in a civil case occasionally present their cases themselves, without the help of a lawyer.

E. The Parties

The parties may or may not be present at the counsel tables with their lawyers. Defendants in criminal cases have a constitutional right to be present. Parties in civil cases may be present if they wish.

F. The Witnesses

Witnesses are individuals who testify under oath about the facts in dispute. When testifying, they sit at the witness stand, facing the courtroom. Because they are asked to testify by one party or the other, they are often referred to as plaintiff's witnesses or defense witnesses.

G. Court Personnel

A court reporter (or sometimes a tape recorder operator) is always present at a trial because federal law requires that a word-for-word record be made of every proceeding. A courtroom deputy clerk, usually seated near the judge, administers the oaths to the witnesses, marks the exhibits, and generally helps keep the trial running smoothly.

H. Adversary Process

Each side presents its most persuasive arguments, emphasizes the facts that support its case, and points out the flaws in its opponent's presentation. According to American judicial tradition, this "adversary process" is the most effective way to help the fact finder arrive at the truth. The jury (or judge, at a bench trial) relies on two types of evidence to decide the case: physical evidence, such as documents and photographs, and the testimony of witnesses.

I. Standards of Proof

In criminal cases, the defendant can be convicted only if the jury (or judge) believes that the government has proven guilt "beyond a reasonable doubt." A jury verdict must be unanimous, meaning that all twelve jurors must vote either "guilty" or "not guilty." The jurors (or judge) must be certain that the defendant committed the crime; they can have no "reasonable doubt" about it. If the jurors cannot agree, the judge declares a mistrial, and the case must be presented to another jury.

In civil cases, the jury or judge decides for the plaintiff if a preponderance of the evidence shows that the defendant failed to perform a legal duty and violated the plaintiff's rights. A "preponderance of the evidence" means that more of the evidence favors the plaintiff's position than favors the defendant's.

J. Admission of Evidence

The federal courts have rules for determining what evidence may be presented in a court proceeding. Sometimes a lawyer tries to present evidence to the jury that may not be proper in light of these rules. The opposing lawyer has a right to object to the questionable evidence, and the judge must decide if it is admissible or not. If the judge rules that the evidence may not be admitted, the opposing lawyer's objection is "sustained." If the judge allows the evidence to be presented, the objection is "overruled."

K. Sentencing

The judge sets a date for a sentencing hearing for criminal defendants who plead guilty or are found guilty at trial. Congress has required judges to base sentences on a system of guidelines that reflect the type of offense and background of the offender. Before the sentencing hearing, a federal probation officer prepares a presentence report to help the judge determine the proper sentence, which can be imprisonment, fines, supervision by a probation officer, or some combination of the three types of sentences.

VIII.   The Appeal Process

The task of the federal courts of appeals and the procedures they follow differ greatly from those of the district courts.

A. Who Can Appeal

A defendant found guilty after a criminal trial and the losing party in a civil trial both have a right to appeal their case to the court of appeals. Appeal is not available to parties who settle a civil suit without trial, or to a criminal defendant who pleads guilty (except that guilty-plea defendants can sometimes appeal their sentences). Appeals are usually based on a claim that the district court made an error either in procedure or in interpreting the law. The government, however, cannot appeal if a criminal defendant is found not guilty. Otherwise, the defendant would be subjected to "double jeopardy," which is forbidden by the Fifth Amendment to the Constitution. The government can appeal in civil cases, as any other party can.

B. Types of Appellate Decisions

A court of appeals can reverse a district court's decision if it finds that the trial judge interpreted the law incorrectly. When the district court is reversed, the case is usually sent back ("remanded") to the district court for further proceedings or another trial. A court of appeals can also affirm a decision of a trial judge and does so in most cases.

C. Appellate Procedure

Courts of appeals usually deliberate in panels of three judges, who decide the case for the entire court. Sometimes, when the parties request it, the entire appeals court will reconsider a panel's decision (called an "en banc" sitting). Courts of appeals review the record (the transcript of the trial and the documents filed in the case), along with written briefs presenting the arguments for both sides. They do not use jurors, witnesses, or court reporters, and the parties are usually not present. The judges may hear oral argument by lawyers in a formal courtroom session, but many cases are decided on the basis of the briefs and the record alone, without oral argument. If oral argument is permitted, the lawyers are given a limited amount of time to explain the case to the judges. The judges frequently ask them questions about their case.

D. Appellate Opinions

The judges on the panel discuss the case in private, consider any relevant prior cases ("precedents"), and reach a decision. At least two of the three judges must agree on the outcome. One judge is chosen to write an opinion, which explains the decision. A judge who disagrees with the majority opinion may file a dissent, giving the reasons for the disagreement. Many appellate opinions are published in books called "reporters," which are read by other judges and by lawyers looking for precedents to guide them in their own cases. The accumulated judicial opinions make up case law, which is usually an accurate predictor of how future cases will be decided.

E. Supreme Court Review

A party who is not satisfied with the decision of the court of appeals may petition the Supreme Court to accept the case for review. Like judges on the courts of appeals, the nine justices on the Supreme Court hear oral arguments, deliberate, render their decisions, and write opinions on cases they decide to review. Unlike the courts of appeals, however, the Supreme Court is not required to hear each case presented to it. It is a different kind of appeals court—its major function is not correcting errors made by trial judges, but clarifying the law when other courts disagree about the interpretation of the Constitution or federal law. Each year the Supreme Court reviews only about 100 of some 7,000 cases that losing parties ask it to review. The Court's decisions in these cases set precedents for the interpretation of the Constitution and federal law that all other federal and state courts must follow.

CHAPTER 2: FEDERAL CRIMINAL PROCEEDINGS

The Court Interpreter's Act provides for the use of interpreters in matters instituted by the United States where the defendant or a witness speaks only or primarily a language other than the English language or suffers from a hearing impairment. Most frequently, this occurs in the context of a criminal case. This section will provide an overview of criminal proceedings in the Federal Courts. Interpreters should fully and accurately interpret everything that is said, either to or from English as required, during the proceeding for which they are providing services.

I.   Arrest and Booking

After being arrested, the defendant is brought to the federal court which has jurisdiction over the matter and is processed. The first step of processing is the booking, and this takes place in the United States Marshal Service's "lock-up."

II.   Interview with Defense Attorney

While awaiting a court appearance, the defendant will meet with an attorney. This may be a retained attorney hired by the defendant, an Assistant Federal Public Defender, or a court appointed Criminal Justice Act (CJA) panel attorney. The interpreter will assist the CJA panel attorney or Public Defender attorney during this interview which could take place in court before the hearing begins or at the United States Marshal Service's "lock-up." Either at this point or right before the initial appearance, the interpreter may be asked to sight translate the charging documents to the defendant.

III.   Pretrial Services Interview

Prior to or very soon after the defendant's initial appearance in court, a pretrial services officer, with the assistance of the interpreter, will interview the defendant concerning his/her background, family status, family ties, friends in the area and the community, education, employment and prior convictions and arrests.

IV.   Initial Appearance

The initial appearance is usually the defendant's first contact with the federal court system in a criminal case.

A. Charges

If possible, the defense is furnished a copy of the complaint in advance of the initial appearance. An interpreter is used at proceedings where the defendant does not comprehend adequately the language in which the proceedings are conducted.

B. Pretrial Release

Pretrial release and detention of criminal defendants are governed by the Eighth Amendment to the United States Constitution ("Excessive bail shall not be required"), and by the Bail Reform Act of 1984, (18 U.S.C. § 3142). In such event, the magistrate judge "shall" impose the least restrictive further condition or combination of conditions that will assure the defendant's appearance and community safety (18 U.S.C. § 3142(c)(1)(B)).

C. Detention Hearing

Pretrial detention may be ordered if, after a detention hearing, the magistrate finds that no condition(s) of release will reasonably assure the defendant's appearance or community safety.

D. Nebbia Hearings

In considering the release of a person on a secured personal or surety bond, the magistrate judge may conduct an inquiry concerning the source of the property to be designated for potential forfeiture or offered as collateral to secure the bond.

V. Preliminary Examination

Unless an indictment has been returned by a grand jury or an information has been filed by the Assistant U.S. Attorney within the time limits set forth in FED R. CRIM. P. 5.1 and 18 U.S.C. § 3060, a defendant who has been charged by complaint is entitled to a preliminary examination before a magistrate judge to determine whether probable cause exists. During the preliminary examination, the magistrate judge will hear testimony from both government witnesses and, in some cases, the defendant. If the magistrate judge finds that there is sufficient evidence to establish probable cause, the defendant is held to answer in the district court. On the other hand, if the magistrate judge determines that the Government has not established probable cause to believe both that an offense has been committed and that the defendant committed it, the pending complaint must be dismissed and the defendant discharged.

A. Grand Jury Proceedings

A grand jury consists of 16 to 23 citizens who are charged by the court to decide whether there is probable cause to require a defendant to stand trial. If so, the grand jury returns an indictment against the defendant. Grand jury proceedings are conducted in secret, and the only people permitted to be present are the grand jury members, the government attorney, the witness under examination, the court reporter, and an interpreter, if required. [3]

VI. Pretrial Preparation and Motions

During the period between the plea and the trial, the attorney will need to interview the defendant. Interpreters may be asked either to go to the jail with the attorney or to the attorney's office if the defendant is on pretrial release. During the interview, interpreters should use the consecutive mode to interpret completely and accurately all questions and statements. Everything said by the attorney and defendant must be interpreted. If interpreters do not understand or hear a statement they must ask that it be repeated rather than leave it out.

---

[3] *How Criminal Cases Move Through District Courts, Part II: Pretrial Proceedings*, JNET, http://jnet.ao.dcn/District/Court_Reporting/Policy_and_Guidance/Federal_Court_System_Overview/How_Criminal _Cases_Move_Through_The_District_Courts/Pretrial_Proceedings.html (last visited March 27, 2013).

A. Pretrial Motions[4]

Sometimes, prior to trial, motions are made by one or both parties requesting a ruling by the court on a matter in dispute. The types of motions that can be made during pretrial proceedings include a discovery motion, a motion to suppress evidence, a motion to sever a matter, a motion based on defects in the indictment or information, and a motion to dismiss the case. If the court must resolve questions of fact in order to rule on the motion, an evidentiary hearing will be held. Interpreters may be required to provide services at these hearings when an LEP defendant is present.

VII. Case Disposition Without Trial: The Guilty Plea

There are cases when a defendant decides to plead guilty rather than go to trial. This often happens after a motion to suppress evidence is denied. The plea of guilty is made before the presiding judicial officer assigned to the case, and in the presence of the assistant United States attorney and the defense attorney.

VIII. Status Conferences

Status conferences consist of determining whether the parties can stipulate to certain facts and whether or not there is a possibility of disposition and, if there is none, in setting a final day for the initiation of the trial, either court trial or jury trial.

IX. Criminal Bench Trials

A criminal bench trial occurs when a defendant waives the right to a trial by jury and consents to be tried by the judge alone, as sole finder of fact. These are often court trials where the judge hears and sees all the evidence and then decides the case by applying the "beyond a reasonable doubt" standard of proof. There can also be bench trials on stipulated facts, i.e., in cases where the parties agree to all or most of the facts of the case and present evidence only as to those facts not included in the stipulation. The court should provide a copy of the joint stipulation of facts to the interpreter in advance of the proceeding.

X. Criminal Jury Trials

A. Impaneling of the Jury

Depending on the type and duration of the case, a jury panel consisting of 30-100 people, is called. The judge questions the jurors during a procedure called voir dire (to speak the truth). The judge may make an unlimited number of juror challenges for cause, such as a juror's inability to decide the case impartially or base a verdict on the evidence alone. The attorneys for both sides also exercise their right to challenge the jurors. Peremptory challenges (challenges without cause) are limited in number for each party. Those jurors who are challenged are excused. The jury selection process must be interpreted simultaneously to the defendant(s). Interpreters may be asked to interpret in chambers or in a separate conference room during the selection process.

---

[4] *Id.*

B. Judge's Initial Jury Instructions

The judge makes a brief statement to the jury concerning basic legal principles, the manner in which the trial is to proceed, the most important duties of the jurors and the behavior of the parties and attorneys toward the jurors. This must be interpreted simultaneously to the defendant(s).

C. Opening Statements

The prosecutor (Assistant United States Attorney) will make an opening statement to the jury. The defense attorney may also make an opening statement, but may waive it or reserve his or her opening statement for later. The opening statement or statements must be interpreted simultaneously to the defendant(s).

D. The Prosecution's Case

It is the government's burden to prove the charges against the defendant beyond a reasonable doubt. The Assistant United States Attorney presents evidence primarily through the examination (testimony) of witnesses. At the end of the government's case, the defense usually presents one or more motions, such as a motion for judgment of acquittal. All arguments, motions, and testimony must be interpreted to the LEP defendant.

E. The Defense Case

If the defense makes no motions mentioned above, or if those motions are denied, the defense presents its case. However, the defendant is not required to present any evidence because the burden of proof always rests with the prosecution and never shifts to the defendant. Then, the same sequence of events applies for the government's case. If the LEP defendant takes the stand, the prosecution may cross-examine the defendant. All testimony must be interpreted using the simultaneous or consecutive modes as appropriate.

F. Rebuttal

Rebuttal is a form of evidence that is presented to contradict or nullify other evidence presented by an adverse party.

G. Closing Arguments

The closing arguments are the final arguments made by the attorneys during the case. In the closing argument, each attorney summarizes the evidence and attempts to persuade the jury to return a verdict in his/her favor. The closing arguments must be interpreted simultaneously to the defendant(s).

H. Jury Instructions

After the closing arguments or summations, the judge instructs the jury as to the law applicable to the case, including the elements of the criminal offense and certain basic legal concepts such as the presumption of innocence and reasonable doubt.

The instructions are to be interpreted to the defendant(s) in the simultaneous mode. Obtaining a copy of the instructions and other written material will help ensure accuracy in the interpretation.

I. Jury Deliberation

Jury deliberation may last any length of time. The jury may request portions of the testimony to be read back by the court reporter, or instructions to be clarified. All read-backs must be interpreted simultaneously for the defendant, unless the defendant's presence has been waived.

J. Verdict

After having deliberated and arrived at a finding, the jury delivers its verdict in open court. The verdict of the jury must be unanimous. Despite the fact that there may have been a break in the proceedings while the jury deliberated, an interpreter must be present to interpret when the jury delivers the verdict. During deliberation, the court may ask the interpreter to remain either in or close to the courthouse, or to provide a contact number at which he or she can be reached.

1. Not Guilty (Acquittal)

The judge discharges the defendant. Bail, if there was any, is exonerated.

2. Guilty

If the defendant is found guilty, a date is set for the sentencing hearing.

3. Hung Jury

If the jury cannot reach a unanimous verdict, the judge declares a mistrial and discharges the jury.

K. Presentence Report

The U.S. probation officer assigned to the case will conduct an investigation of the defendant's background and will conduct an interview with the defendant and sometimes also with the defendant's family or friends. If the defendant is a LEP individual, an interpreter will be assigned to assist and will interpret everything that is said using the consecutive mode.

L. Sentencing Hearing

The sentencing hearing in many cases is a lengthy evidentiary hearing, and sometimes the testimony of witnesses is taken. Interpreters will use the simultaneous mode for arguments and discussions and the consecutive mode for testimony during questions and answers. After the sentence is imposed, the judge advises the convicted defendant of appeal rights.

XI.   Misdemeanor Cases

Misdemeanors are offenses punishable by a term of imprisonment of one year or less. Petty offenses and infractions are subcategories of misdemeanors. A defendant charged with a misdemeanor may elect to be tried before either a magistrate judge or a district judge. In order to be tried before a United States magistrate judge, the defendant must sign a written consent which specifically waives the right to trial, judgment and sentencing before a district judge. Consents to proceed before the magistrate judge are obtained in virtually all cases.

XII.   Group Hearings and Multiple Defendant Cases

It is the responsibility of the Court to provide interpreters in multiple-defendant criminal actions and multiple-party civil actions initiated by the United States. Courts may also choose to place multiple defendants facing the same or similar charges or material witnesses into small groups for hearings. A clear line should be drawn between group hearings, which are common even in smaller courts and via the Telephone Interpreting Program (TIP), and hearings that are held en masse. Group hearings are handled in a manner which allows the Court to address the defendants in the group individually. Questions, answers or comments made by the defendants are also heard individually.

Wireless interpreting equipment is highly recommended for in-person group hearings and multiple phone headsets are required for hearings covered by TIP. The interpreter must ensure that all individuals in a group are able to hear the interpretation at all times. It is also important that all individuals in the group be close to a microphone so the interpreter and the court can hear any answer or question they may have for the Court.

It is recommended that the Court or the interpreter explain to the individuals in the group how the interpretation process will work and the order in which they are to answer. A quick orientation will prevent all defendants from answering at once or out of order. Having individual answers will guarantee a clear record and facilitate interpretation.

CHAPTER 3: OVERVIEW OF COURT INTERPRETING

Court interpreters are considered officers of the court with the specific duty and responsibility of interpreting between the languages specified. Interpreters help ensure access to justice by facilitating the full participation of LEP individuals in the judicial process.

I.   Interpreter Skills

Although the federal courts make extensive use of written documents, court interpreters deal primarily in the oral rendition of speech from one language into another during the course of judicial proceedings. Interpretation differs from translation, which is the transfer of written words from one language to another. Interpretation can also be the transfer of discourse from verbal to sign (symbol) language and vice versa. Sight translation involves rendering written text from the source language orally into the target language.

Interpretation goes beyond having the ability to speak two languages. Interpreters must possess mastery of the source and target languages, as well as interpreting skills. Courts will often verify an interpreter's credentials on the record, through a structured voir dire process. Professional interpreter organizations and linguistic experts identify the following aspects needed for effective interpreting:

- Comprehensive knowledge of the source and target language.
- Ability to listen, comprehend, and discern the message conveyed in the source language.
- Ability to grasp and maintain communication logic and distinguish between primary and secondary points.
- Technical ability for short-term memory, simultaneous listening and note-taking.
- Well-developed vocabulary, specialized terminology, and general knowledge of many subject areas.
- Message production, good diction, and pronunciation.
- Knowledge and experience of varying dialects, colloquialisms, regionalisms and cultural differences.
- Ability to conserve language register (formal to formal and informal to informal) for a variety of speakers with divergent educational backgrounds.
- Knowledge of idiomatic expressions in both languages.
- A well-developed sense of professionalism and respect for ethical considerations.

II.   Language Skills

Professional interpreters have a mastery of at least two languages (source and target), excellent skills in the principal modes of interpretation (simultaneous and consecutive), extensive knowledge of the subject matter vocabularies in question, plus mental and physical stamina. Court interpreters are highly skilled language specialists who perform sight translation, simultaneous, and consecutive interpretation. They convert the words of the speaker to the language of the listener. Interpreters are never the authors of the speech, but they must grasp the meaning and style of discourse rapidly, find an equivalent in another language, and articulate it. A common error is the belief that any person who knows two languages can interpret.

While court interpreting may appear to be a field that primarily requires knowledge of legal vocabulary, the subject matter to be interpreted is often quite diverse. In an average criminal trial, sophisticated legal arguments will be interpreted, as well as the testimony of handwriting, ballistics, fingerprint, chemical, DNA, and drug experts. Interpreters must have a broad active and passive vocabulary and an excellent knowledge of regionalisms, idioms and dialectical variations of the countries in which their language is spoken. Court interpreters must have these variations of language readily available due to the diversity of witnesses and defendants.

III. Modes of Interpretation

A. Simultaneous

Simultaneous interpretation is a running rendition of everything said in the source language into the target language. Simultaneous interpretation requires that interpreters listen and speak almost concurrently with the primary speaker whose words are being translated. In effect, interpreters are simultaneously performing two tasks in the field of language communication that are otherwise practiced separately: speech and understanding.

It is important to note that interpreters are not performing word-for-word translation, but transferring thoughts and ideas accurately and completely from a source to a target language. Concentrated listening is crucial for an exact rendering of the original message; thus, the importance of adequate listening conditions, acoustics, correct usage of microphones by speakers, and availability of appropriate equipment.

B. Consecutive

Consecutive interpretation is the "question and answer" mode in which the speaker completes a statement and the interpreter begins to interpret after the statement is completed. The consecutive mode is most often utilized with witnesses on the stand. Traditionally, consecutive interpreting has been divided into long and short versions. While the long method is generally reserved for some forms of conference interpreting, the short method is preferred in the legal setting because it emphasizes the verbatim rendition required in legal proceedings. Short consecutive is a mode by which interpreters relay a message in the target language in a sequential manner after the speaker. Several unique considerations and skills come into play when consecutive interpreting is used. These include:

I. Length of Testimony

Although the speaker may make natural pauses during testimony to allow for the interpretation, this is not always the case. At times, due to the complexity or excessive length of an utterance, interpreters may not be able to retain the complete message and will need the speaker to pause. Defense attorneys and prosecutors, when posing questions during direct or cross-examination, should pause at appropriate intervals. This will enable the interpreter to accurately and completely render the words into the target language.

II.   Interrupting the Speaker

When the need for an interruption arises, interpreters should gently signal to the speaker to pause. This may be accomplished through a hand gesture, a nod of the head, or eye contact. On occasion, such a signal may not be sufficient, in which case interpreters must interrupt the speaker.

III.   Note-Taking

Interpreters should always be prepared to take notes when interpreting. It is strongly recommended that dates, numbers, proper names, lists, addresses, etc., be written down. Note-taking should be simple, individualized and designed to assist memory.

IV.   Gestures and Emotions

When a witness makes hand gestures, i.e., indicating distances or size, interpreters should refrain from attempting to duplicate these gestures since it is impossible to preserve accuracy in such instances. Interpreters should always strive to maintain a professional demeanor and should be aware not to call unnecessary attention by making gestures or facial expressions while interpreting.

Studies of court interpreted proceedings conducted by Dr. Susan Berk-Seligson[5] have found that jurors' impressions of the defendant or witness are affected by the actions and demeanor of the interpreter. In her studies, which included actual and simulated court proceedings, she found that the unconscious manipulation of grammatical forms or modification of speech styles of witnesses, lengthening or shortening testimony, politeness, hedging and level of formality used by the interpreter were factors which influenced jurors.

V.   Mathematical Conversions

As a rule, interpreters must not make mathematical conversions or measurements; i.e., foreign currency denominations, meters into yards, kilos into pounds and so on.

VI.   Corrections by Interpreter

If the interpreter makes a mistake on the stand, it should be noted immediately by the interpreter to the presiding judicial officer for the record, or as soon as he/she becomes aware of the mistake.

C. Sight Translation

Sight translation is conveying orally in one language the words of a text written in another language. It is a hybrid of translation and interpretation that requires the interpreter to first review the original written text, and then render it orally into the other language. The interpreter needs to read the entire text before rendering a sight translation in open court. The

---

[5] SUSAN BERK-SELIGSON, THE BILINGUAL COURTROOM: COURT INTERPRETERS IN THE JUDICIAL PROCESS (1st ed. 1990).

interpreter should inform the Court if additional time is needed to review the document before being able to render an accurate sight translation into the record.

IV. Accuracy of Performance

Interpreters must provide language services with accuracy and precision to help ensure due process for all defendants in criminal proceedings. The basic notion of fairness mandates that all defendants be fully and immediately informed of the testimony as it occurs. The accuracy of court interpretation may have a direct impact upon the decisions made during both criminal and civil proceedings. The potentially grave consequences of inaccurate legal interpretation mandate that great skill and caution be utilized by interpreters.

An important component of accuracy is the interpreter's ability to avoid the use of summary interpretation and provide a complete rendition of everything that is said into the target language. Summary interpretation involves paraphrasing or condensing the speaker's statement, thereby omitting some portion of what was said.[6] Such omissions are contrary to the interpreter's duty to render the speaker's complete message. Summary interpretation is not acceptable in legal proceedings because it improperly substitute's the interpreter's judgment as to which parts of a statement or testimony are most important and shifts the interpreter from their role as an impartial conduit to an active participant in the matter.

The conditions and circumstances of performing in a courtroom make the court interpreter's task of maintaining accuracy especially arduous. Unlike conference interpreters, who only have to concentrate on one speaker at a time and are generally given time to prepare in advance, court interpreters must concentrate on many speakers in a short time frame and preserve the style, language level, idiosyncrasies, idioms and other aspects of each speaker and speech pattern.

The poor acoustical quality of some courtrooms is often a vexing aspect of simultaneous court interpreting. Except in unusual circumstances, interpreters have no amplified audio support and they must often perform in oversized courtrooms without public address systems. Interpreters may find that loud, clear speech is not always delivered in courtrooms. Therefore, much interpreting will be performed while trying to decipher what has been said by someone whose back is toward the interpreter, whose voice may be low, and/or whose sentences are dropping off inaudibly. Court interpreters must hear and understand an argument or testimony while converting the words into the language of the LEP individual. Whenever possible, speakers should avoid facing away from the interpreter and use a microphone, being especially careful to remain within range of it. Since simultaneous interpreters have only a few seconds to spare, poor audibility is a major obstacle to accurate performance. If impediments to an accurate performance occur, the interpreter should bring them to the attention of the judge as respectfully and as unobtrusively as possible. By way of example, in the case of a soft-spoken party, it is helpful to rise and say, "Your Honor, the interpreter is having a hard time hearing", and in the case of a party who speaks or reads too quickly, "Your Honor, the interpreter is having a hard time keeping up."

---

[6] ARLENE M. KELLY, NAT'L ASS'N OF JUDICIARY INTERPRETERS & TRANSLATORS, SUMMARY INTERPRETING IN LEGAL SETTINGS 1 (2005).

Among the measures that a court may implement to help interpreters operate at a high level of proficiency are:

1. Use multiple interpreters for lengthy or complex proceedings such as trials and evidentiary hearings, legal arguments on motions, and sentencing hearings with complex issues. See the Guide to Judiciary Policy, Volume 5, Chapter 5, §530.30.

2. Interpreters should vary position occasionally, e.g., combining sitting and standing beside the witness stand, if doing so will not interfere with the hearing.

3. The court should provide the interpreter drinking water and sufficient space in which to write and keep reference material. This could be either at a separate table or at the counsel table, if available. Courts should also provide all proper interpreting equipment that is available.

4. The court should provide attorneys with general guidance as to the demands that an interpreted proceeding will impose on them and other courtroom participants. This includes the use of sound equipment, the need to speak clearly, the position of the interpreter in the courtroom, the need to change interpreters periodically during lengthy proceedings, the possibility of interruption by the interpreter in order to clarify a matter, and the avoidance of social and ex parte contact with interpreters, etc.

V.   Ethical Obligations

In addition to language considerations, court interpreters must always comply with certain ethical constraints and rules that are not binding on interpreters in other fields, such as escort and conference interpreting. Court interpreters must remain and appear independent of the defendants or witnesses, even though seated right next to them throughout lengthy proceedings. A simple conversation about the weather can be misinterpreted by English-only speaking jurors.

VI.   Language Style and Register

The principal aim of interpreters is to give as exact a rendition as possible, using direct speech. This is true whether the language is nonsensical, fragmented and contradictory; or whether it is erudite, philosophical and highly technical discourse. Interpreters are tasked with remaining unobtrusive, so that the fact finders can concentrate on the witness rather than the interpreters.

VII.   Interpreters in the Courtroom

A. Location of Interpreters in Court

The interpreter should be located at a site in the courtroom where he or she can clearly hear and see the defendant, the witness, counsel, and the presiding judicial officer at all times. Normally, the most desirable location is between the witness stand and the defense table. Bulky objects should not be placed on the stand to block the interpreter's view of the witness. If the place of examination should shift from the witness stand, the interpreter should be able to follow the parties elsewhere in the courtroom in order to see and hear the speaker. See Appendix 6 for more information.

B. Aids to the Interpreter

Suitable accommodations should be accessible to the interpreter if available, examples include: a chair at the witness stand, a chair at counsel table, and a glass of drinking water. There should be sufficient space in the courtroom for the interpreter to have a reasonable amount of material (i.e., glossary, dictionary) nearby for immediate reference. Additionally, many courts may have policies allowing interpreters in the courtroom to utilize electronic dictionaries, internet enabled tablet devices, or laptop computers for access to reference materials. Interpreters should check the local court rules to determine if and when they may use any of these types of resources while in the courtroom.

C. Number of Interpreters per Proceeding: Team/Tandem Interpreting

The number of interpreters may vary according to the type and complexity of the proceeding and the availability of equipment for the number of defendants that require interpreting services. To mitigate the effects of interpreter fatigue and safeguard the integrity of interpreting services, long and/or complex proceedings may be covered by two interpreters through team, or tandem interpreting. See Guide to Judiciary Policy, Volume 5, Chapter 5, §530. When team interpreting is used, the passive interpreter should remain seated in close proximity to the active interpreter and refrain from leaving the courtroom for any significant length of time without good reason.

It is the duty of each member of a team to provide the other member(s) with all support necessary to ensure the accuracy of the interpretation in a manner consistent with the dignity and decorum of a court of law. The passive interpreter should be ready to whisper words or pass a written note to the active interpreter in case a lapse of memory or other issue arises. The passive interpreter should take care of any problems arising with the equipment the team uses and write down things such as names, addresses, and other numbers that come up, making them available for easy visual reference by the active interpreter. This reduces the amount of attention that the active interpreter must pay to things other than the interpreting task. Where necessary, the passive interpreter should research terminology for the active interpreter.

D. Challenges and Corrections to Interpretation

When the interpreter first begins to interpret at the witness stand, the presiding judicial officer will generally identify the court interpreter as a neutral party and explain that the interpreter's rendition in English will be the record, rather than the utterance by the LEP individual. Even if the presiding judicial officer does not make a formal statement to this effect, the interpreter should still interpret the proceeding from a neutral perspective, regardless of any expectations which may be held by the parties to the case.

Should an attorney appropriately correct the interpretation, the interpreter should state "the interpreter stands corrected" followed by the correct word or phrase. When not in agreement with the correction, the interpreter should state "the interpreter stands by the interpretation." Because there is the possibility for mistrial in a situation where the interpretation is challenged, and because the interpreter must endeavor never to be the cause of a mistrial, it is important for the interpreter to create a clear record to either correct or support the rendition that is challenged. A record to support the interpretation will reflect: (1) the question by the attorney; (2) the answer by the witness; (3) the objection by the attorney; and (4) a corrected answer by the witness. In any discussion that develops as a result of the challenge, the interpreter should address only the presiding judicial officer, not the attorneys.

A challenge from the defendant or a witness should be handled in much the same manner as above. A simple statement of correction or support by the interpreter should suffice. In any discussion, interpreters should address only the presiding judicial officer. Under certain circumstances, interpreters may request an opportunity to clarify the word or phrase at issue with the defendant/witness. This request should be made openly on the record. It should be followed by a statement of correction or support.

A correction requested by the presiding judicial officer should be tactfully handled in the same manner as a correction from any other source. Interpreters either should correct or support the interpretation for the record.

Corrections and disputes among team interpreters over interpretation should be handled privately and quietly, involving the court only if it is deemed necessary. If a correction is felt necessary, it should be whispered to the active interpreter or written down on a note passed only to that interpreter. Corrections to the interpretation should be handled in a professional, courteous manner, as soon as practically possible without disrupting the proceedings.

VIII.   Simultaneous Interpretation of Recorded Audio

At a hearing or trial, interpreters may occasionally be requested to simultaneously interpret the contents of an audio file on the record. Whenever possible, interpreters should refrain from providing this type of on-the-spot simultaneous interpretation of audio recordings.[7] Interpretations of audio recordings under these circumstances will often not meet appropriate evidentiary standards due to poor sound quality, lack of preparation and research time, and lack of proper courtroom technology.[8]

In the event that the interpreter is ordered to perform this task, there are a few guidelines that should be followed. First, "the interpreter should make it clear to all parties that an immediate rendition of the material in question will likely fail to meet the high standards" of the interpreter's oath, which "mandates faithfulness and accuracy to the best of the interpreter's ability."[9] While rendering the interpretation, interpreters must refrain from making any comments or gestures indicating approval, disapproval, or opinion as to the accuracy of the transcribed translation in question, or in any way interfering with the playing of the recording. If asked or consulted in open court on the accuracy of a transcribed translation, interpreters should withhold expressing an opinion until reasonably sure of having sufficient time and opportunity to review the recording in question. Interpreters should also refrain from expressing a professional opinion outside the courtroom since terms taken out of context may vary in meaning.

---

[7] *See generally* TERESA C. SALAZAR & GLADYS SEGAL, NAT'L ASS'N OF JUDICIARY INTERPRETERS & TRANSLATORS, ONSITE SIMULTANEOUS TRANSLATION OF A SOUND FILE IS NOT RECOMMENDED 1-3 (2006).

[8] *Id.*

[9] *Id.* at 2.

CHAPTER 4: INTERPRETER SUPERVISION AND CONTRACTING

I.   Orientation of Interpreters

Sufficient orientation should be provided to new or inexperienced staff and contract court interpreters to enable them to serve effectively and without undue stress. The study of certain chapters of this manual, a tour of the courtroom, review of the case materials and a brief conversation with the defendant or witness may be useful when preparing for the assignment. Additional in-depth orientation about the court and case may also be necessary. Interpreters should also inquire about the location and usage of any available interpretation equipment or resources that the court may have.

Interpreters from outside the federal courts, in spite of their interpreting experience, may not have a sufficient understanding of the legal terminology, procedure, protocol, demeanor and the duties and responsibilities of the federal court interpreter. Similarly, while experience as an interpreter in state court may be helpful to the interpreter, the differences between the two systems are significant and may be confusing. Guidance in this area should be available to the interpreter wherever possible. For example, measures should be taken to ensure that interpreters are aware of the type of proceeding assigned. This will assist them in determining the relevant terminology likely to be encountered and also help the LEP defendant/witness to understand the nature of the proceeding. Additionally, inexperienced interpreters should be made familiar with the proper role and function of interpreters in the court proceeding, so as to guard against unwanted personal interaction with the defendant or witnesses, or other considerations such as being unobtrusive and advance preparation for future assignments.

II.   Administration of Oath

Each interpreter takes an oath to properly discharge role and responsibilities of an interpreter, including interpreting accurately for the speakers in the proceeding and preparing properly for the assignment. In some courts, the duty of swearing the interpreter is delegated to the courtroom clerk.

Policies with regard to the oath of interpreters vary from court to court. In some, contract interpreters are sworn each day before court convenes. In others, administering the oath at the beginning of a proceeding is sufficient for the entire case, regardless of duration. Some districts keep a detailed, written oath on file, which is executed during the orientation process in order to dispense with the need to swear the interpreter in before each individual hearing.

III.   Staff Interpreters

Staff interpreters are employees of the Office of the Clerk of Court. When a staff court interpreter has no case preparation or in-court work to perform, the clerk may assign other duties that take advantage of bilingual skills, such as telephone and over-the-counter assistance to non-English speakers. At the discretion of the clerk, staff interpreters may also be assigned to assist other courts through the Telephone Interpreting Program (TIP), if the court has the equipment necessary to provide this service. This practice is encouraged, results in cost savings to the judiciary, and also helps ensure that federally certified court interpreters are available when needed.

IV. Contract Court Interpreters

A contract court interpreter is not an employee of the court, but is an independent contractor used for short durations to provide interpreting services. Contract court interpreters may be AO certified or otherwise qualified interpreters. For more information on interpreter certification and qualifications, see Appendix 4 of this document and the *Guide to Judiciary Policy, Volume 5, Chapter 3*.

A. Terms and Conditions

Once a contract court interpreter has been identified for an event, his or her classification, qualifications, and suitability have been determined, and terms negotiated, the court must provide the interpreter with a completed Contract for Court Interpreter Services, comprising Part I, Terms and Conditions, and Part II, the Rate and Information Sheet. The Rate and Information Sheet must be signed by the interpreter and the original returned to the court to indicate that the interpreter has agreed to comply with the rates and information indicated in the Contract for Court Interpreter Services document. The Contracting Officer should ensure that the interpreter is given a copy of the contract with both signatures on it. A copy of the current Terms and Conditions for contract court interpreters can be found online by following the link at http://www.uscourts.gov/FederalCourts/UnderstandingtheFederalCourts/DistrictCourts/Court Interpreters.aspx.

B. FBI Background Checks

All interpreters who wish to work for the federal courts must be fingerprinted and submit to an FBI background check. The first court to use an interpreter who has not had an FBI background check should initiate the background check; however, any federal court may request the background check. Background check information provided by the FBI to the AO is viewable only by appointing officials and their chief deputies with a specific need for the information.

C. Fees for Daily Work

The approved maximum daily fees for AO certified, professionally qualified and language-skilled interpreters are set out in the Director's Fee Schedule, which is updated periodically. Daily fees should be negotiated between the contract court interpreter and the court prior to completing the Contract for Court Interpreter Services. Contract court interpreter rates are based on a half-day/full-day scale.

The AO provides a standard Contract for Court Interpreter Services, which includes two parts. Part I is the standard Terms and Conditions which should be used by the courts in their contracts with interpreters. Part II is the Rate and Information Sheet which must be personalized for each interpreter with the negotiated terms and conditions of payment and reimbursement. The regulations in the Guide to Judiciary Policy pertaining to court interpreters may be incorporated in the contract by reference.

Interpreters whose services are authorized under the Criminal Justice Act (CJA), 18 U.S.C. § 3006A, and related statutes to facilitate communication between counsel and the defendant out-of-court are generally paid under the CJA. Therefore, the rates set forth in the Director's Fee Schedule are not mandatory in these instances, and the interpreter should negotiate the fee (utilizing the Fee Schedule, hourly rates, or other appropriate basis) with the CJA attorney. Unless unusual circumstances exist, however, the rate paid to interpreters pursuant to subsection (e) of the CJA should not exceed the rates provided by the Director's Fee Schedule or the presumptive or maximum rates adopted by a court. See the Guide to Judiciary Policy, Volume 5, Chapter 2, § 220.10 and Guide to Judiciary Policy, Volume 7A, § 320.15.10 and 320.15.20.

D. Travel and Expenses

Contract court interpreters who are required to travel beyond the local commuting distance in the performance of their assigned duties are entitled to reimbursement in accordance with the Judiciary Staff Travel Regulations set out in the Guide to Judiciary Policy, Volume 19, Chapter 4. The local commuting distance to the courthouse is set at the discretion of each court, but it is typically an area within a 30 mile radius of the courthouse. Travel expenses within the local commuting distance have already been considered by the AO in setting the rates in the Director's Fee Schedule.

Contract court interpreters may only claim reimbursement for subsistence expenses on an actual expense (itemized) basis, with receipts for lodging and for any expense of more than $25, up to the GSA per diem rate for the date and location. Time spent traveling will generally be compensated at the daily rate of pay, i.e., minimum of a half-day fee for same day travel outside of the local commuting distance when in-court time does not exceed 4 hours.

Expenses other than ordinary travel and subsistence should be avoided if possible. The clerk should inform the contract interpreter in advance of the policy regarding such expenses. An interpreter's rental of equipment for multiple-party interpretation cannot be reimbursed.

E. Procedures for Payment

As noted in the Guide to Judiciary Policy, the interpreter must submit an invoice for services. The Terms and Conditions for Contract Court Interpreter Services, Section 7.1 specifies that an original invoice and/or local court form for services rendered shall be submitted by the interpreter within 30 days of completion of a given assignment to the address indicated for invoices in the Rate and Information Sheet. If the interpreter is entitled to travel subsistence, an AO Form 1012, Travel Voucher, should be completed and attached. Copies of forms should be given to the interpreter at the beginning of the proceeding, usually as part of the orientation to the court. If the interpreter is to be paid during the course of a lengthy proceeding for an assignment that extends beyond one month, the contract court interpreter may submit an interim invoice. Payment may not be provided before the work is performed.

F. CJA Voucher Processing

In cases where the Office of the Clerk is charged with processing CJA interpreter vouchers, the clerk must be familiar with the statutory provisions regarding expert or other services. Limits are placed on the amounts that may be paid without advance judicial approval; limits also apply with respect to approval of the payment claim by the chief judge of the circuit court of appeals (or delegate circuit judge) and advance approval of the chief circuit judge may also be recommended or required. Since the specific fee allowances fluctuate periodically as a result of statutory changes, the clerk should refer to the Guidelines for Administering the CJA and Related Statutes, Volume 7A, Guide to Judiciary Policy, for current information. The relevant voucher is CJA Form 21, Authorization and Voucher for Expert and other Services or CJA Form 31, Death Penalty Proceedings: Ex Parte Request For Authorization and Voucher For Expert and Other Services. These limits do not apply and these vouchers are not used when a federal defender organization retains the services of an interpreter.

Appendix 1: The Court Interpreters Act

28 U.S.C. §1827 – Interpreters in courts of the United States

(a) The Director of the Administrative Office of the United States Courts shall establish a program to facilitate the use of certified and otherwise qualified interpreters in judicial proceedings instituted by the United States.

(b)

(1) The Director shall prescribe, determine, and certify the qualifications of persons who may serve as certified interpreters, when the Director considers certification of interpreters to be merited, for the hearing impaired (whether or not also speech impaired) and persons who speak only or primarily a language other than the English language, in judicial proceedings instituted by the United States. The Director may certify interpreters for any language if the Director determines that there is a need for certified interpreters in that language. Upon the request of the Judicial Conference of the United States for certified interpreters in a language, the Director shall certify interpreters in that language. Upon such a request from the judicial council of a circuit and the approval of the Judicial Conference, the Director shall certify interpreters for that circuit in the language requested. The judicial council of a circuit shall identify and evaluate the needs of the districts within a circuit. The Director shall certify interpreters based on the results of criterion-referenced performance examinations. The Director shall issue regulations to carry out this paragraph within 1 year after the date of the enactment of the Judicial Improvements and Access to Justice Act.

(2) Only in a case in which no certified interpreter is reasonably available as provided in subsection (d) of this section, including a case in which certification of interpreters is not provided under paragraph (1) in a particular language, may the services of otherwise qualified interpreters be used. The Director shall provide guidelines to the courts for the selection of otherwise qualified interpreters, in order to ensure that the highest standards of accuracy are maintained in all judicial proceedings subject to the provisions of this chapter.

(3) The Director shall maintain a current master list of all certified interpreters and otherwise qualified interpreters and shall report periodically on the use and performance of both certified and otherwise qualified interpreters in judicial proceedings instituted by the United States and on the languages for which interpreters have been certified. The Director shall prescribe, subject to periodic review, a schedule of reasonable fees for services rendered by interpreters, certified or otherwise, used in proceedings instituted by the United States, and in doing so shall consider the prevailing rate of compensation for comparable service in other governmental entities.

(c)

(1) Each United States district court shall maintain on file in the office of the clerk, and each United States attorney shall maintain on file, a list of all persons who have been certified as interpreters by the Director in accordance with subsection (b) of this section. The clerk shall make the list of certified interpreters for judicial proceeding available upon request.

(2) The clerk of the court, or other court employee designated by the chief judge, shall be responsible for securing the services of certified interpreters and otherwise qualified interpreters required for proceedings initiated by the United States, except that the United States attorney is responsible for securing the services of such interpreters for governmental witnesses.

(d)

(1) The presiding judicial officer, with the assistance of the Director of the Administrative Office of the United States Courts, shall utilize the services of the most available certified interpreter, or when no certified interpreter is reasonably available, as determined by the presiding judicial officer, the services of an otherwise qualified interpreter, in judicial proceedings instituted by the United States, if the presiding judicial officer determines on such officer's own motion or on the motion of a party that such party (including a defendant in a criminal case), or a witness who may present testimony in such judicial proceedings—

    (A) speaks only or primarily a language other than the English language; or

    (B) suffers from a hearing impairment (whether or not suffering also from a speech impairment)

so as to inhibit such party's comprehension of the proceedings or communication with counsel or the presiding judicial officer, or so as to inhibit such witness' comprehension of questions and the presentation of such testimony.

(2) Upon the motion of a party, the presiding judicial officer shall determine whether to require the electronic sound recording of a judicial proceeding in which an interpreter is used under this section. In making this determination, the presiding judicial officer shall consider, among other things, the qualifications of the interpreter and prior experience in interpretation of court proceedings; whether the language to be interpreted is not one of the languages for which the Director has certified interpreters, and the complexity or length of the proceeding. In a grand jury proceeding, upon the motion of the accused, the presiding judicial officer shall require the electronic sound recording of the portion of the proceeding in which an interpreter is used.

(e)

    (1) If any interpreter is unable to communicate effectively with the presiding judicial officer, the United States attorney, a party (including a defendant in a criminal case), or a witness, the presiding judicial officer shall dismiss such interpreter and obtain the services of another interpreter in accordance with this section.

    (2) In any judicial proceedings instituted by the United States, if the presiding judicial officer does not appoint an interpreter under subsection (d) of this section, an individual requiring the services of an interpreter may seek assistance of the clerk of court or the Director of the Administrative Office of the United States Courts in obtaining the assistance of a certified interpreter.

(f)

    (1) Any individual other than a witness who is entitled to interpretation under subsection (d) of this section may waive such interpretation in whole or in part. Such a waiver shall be effective only if approved by the presiding judicial officer and made expressly by such individual on the record after opportunity to consult with counsel and after the presiding judicial officer has explained to such individual, utilizing the services of the most available certified interpreter, or when no certified interpreter is reasonably available, as determined by the presiding judicial officer, the services of an otherwise competent interpreter, the nature and effect of the waiver.

    (2) An individual who waives under paragraph (1) of this subsection the right to an interpreter may utilize the services of a noncertified interpreter of such individual's choice whose fees, expenses, and costs shall be paid in the manner provided for the payment of such fees, expenses, and costs of an interpreter appointed under subsection (d) of this section.

(g)

    (1) There are authorized to be appropriated to the Federal judiciary, and to be paid by the Director of the Administrative Office of the United States Courts, such sums as may be necessary to establish a program to facilitate the use of certified and otherwise qualified interpreters, and otherwise fulfill the provisions of this section and the Judicial Improvements and Access to Justice Act, except as provided in paragraph (3).

    (2) Implementation of the provisions of this section is contingent upon the availability of appropriated funds to carry out the purposes of this section.

    (3) Such salaries, fees, expenses, and costs that are incurred with respect to Government witnesses (including for grand jury proceedings) shall, unless direction is made under paragraph (4), be paid by the Attorney General from sums appropriated to the Department of Justice.

(4) Upon the request of any person in any action for which interpreting services established pursuant to subsection (d) are not otherwise provided, the clerk of the court, or other court employee designated by the chief judge, upon the request of the presiding judicial officer, shall, where possible, make such services available to that person on a cost-reimbursable basis, but the judicial officer may also require the prepayment of the estimated expenses of providing such services.

(5) If the Director of the Administrative Office of the United States Courts finds it necessary to develop and administer criterion-referenced performance examinations for purposes of certification, or other examinations for the selection of otherwise qualified interpreters, the Director may prescribe for each examination a uniform fee for applicants to take such examination. In determining the rate of the fee for each examination, the Director shall consider the fees charged by other organizations for examinations that are similar in scope or nature. Notwithstanding section 3302 (b) of title 31, the Director is authorized to provide in any contract or agreement for the development or administration of examinations and the collection of fees that the contractor may retain all or a portion of the fees in payment for the services. Notwithstanding paragraph (6) of this subsection, all fees collected after the effective date of this paragraph and not retained by a contractor shall be deposited in the fund established under section 1931 of this title and shall remain available until expended.

(6) Any moneys collected under this subsection may be used to reimburse the appropriations obligated and disbursed in payment for such services.

(h) The presiding judicial officer shall approve the compensation and expenses payable to interpreters, pursuant to the schedule of fees prescribed by the Director under subsection (b)(3).

(i) The term "presiding judicial officer" as used in this section refers to any judge of a United States district court, including a bankruptcy judge, a United States magistrate judge, and in the case of grand jury proceedings conducted under the auspices of the United States attorney, a United States attorney.

(j) The term "judicial proceedings instituted by the United States" as used in this section refers to all proceedings, whether criminal or civil, including pretrial and grand jury proceedings (as well as proceedings upon a petition for a writ of habeas corpus initiated in the name of the United States by a relator) conducted in, or pursuant to the lawful authority and jurisdiction of a United States district court. The term "United States district court" as used in this subsection includes any court which is created by an Act of Congress in a territory and is invested with any jurisdiction of a district court established by chapter 5 of this title.

(k) The interpretation provided by certified or otherwise qualified interpreters pursuant to this section shall be in the simultaneous mode for any party to a judicial proceeding instituted by the United States and in the consecutive mode for witnesses, except that the presiding judicial officer, sua sponte or on the motion of a party, may authorize a simultaneous, or consecutive interpretation when such officer determines after a hearing on the record that such interpretation will aid in the efficient administration of justice. The presiding judicial officer, on such officer's motion or on the motion of a party, may order that special interpretation services as authorized in section 1828 of this title be provided if such officer determines that the provision of such services will aid in the efficient administration of justice.

(l) Notwithstanding any other provision of this section or section 1828, the presiding judicial officer may appoint a certified or otherwise qualified sign language interpreter to provide services to a party, witness, or other participant in a judicial proceeding, whether or not the proceeding is instituted by the United States, if the presiding judicial officer determines, on such officer's own motion or on the motion of a party or other participant in the proceeding, that such individual suffers from a hearing impairment. The presiding judicial officer shall, subject to the availability of appropriated funds, approve the compensation and expenses payable to sign language interpreters appointed under this section in accordance with the schedule of fees prescribed by the Director under subsection (b)(3) of this section.

APPENDIX 2: VOLUME 5 OF THE GUIDE TO JUDICIARY POLICY

The *Guide to Judiciary Policy* serves as "a repository of the federal judiciary's administrative policies, as determined by the Judicial Conference of the United States or the Director of the Administrative Office, or as mandated by statute or other legal requirement," see Guide to Judiciary Policy, Vol 1, § 110.

The *Guide to Judiciary Policy, Volume 5: Court Interpreting* deals specifically with policy related to the court interpreting program. It provides policy guidance on a variety of interpreting topics, such as qualifications, contracting and payment, appointment authorities, and definitions. The Chapter headings within Volume 5 include:

- Chapter 1: Overview
- Chapter 2: Appointment and Payment Authorities
- Chapter 3: Court Management and Responsibility
- Chapter 4: Funding, Contracting, and Paying
- Chapter 5: Special Interpretation Services

Volume 5 is available on the judiciary's public website at http://www.uscourts.gov/uscourts/FederalCourts/Publications/Guide_Vol05.pdf.

APPENDIX 3: COURT INTERPRETER ETHICS AND PROTOCOL

Standards for Performance and Professional Responsibility for Contract Court Interpreters in the Federal Courts[10]

Preamble

Federally certified court interpreters are highly skilled professionals who bring to the judicial process specialized language skills, impartiality, and propriety in dealing with parties, counsel, the court, and the jury. All contract court interpreters, regardless of certification, are appointed to serve the court pursuant to 28 U.S.C. § 1827. When interpreters are sworn in they become, for the duration of the assignment, officers of the court with the specific duty and responsibility of interpreting between English and the language specified. In their capacity as officers of the court, contract court interpreters are expected to follow the Standards for Performance and Professional Responsibility for Contract Court Interpreters in the Federal Courts.

1: Accuracy and Completeness

Interpreters shall render a complete and accurate interpretation or sight translation that preserves the level of language used without altering, omitting, or adding anything to what is stated or written, and without explanation. The obligation to preserve accuracy includes the interpreter's duty to correct any error of interpretation discovered by the interpreter during the proceeding.

2: Representation of Qualifications

Interpreters shall accurately and completely represent their certifications, training, and pertinent experience.

3: Impartiality, Conflicts of Interest, and Remuneration and Gifts

Impartiality. Interpreters shall be impartial and unbiased and shall refrain from conduct that may give an appearance of bias. During the course of the proceedings, interpreters shall not converse with parties, witnesses, jurors, attorneys, or with friends or relatives of any party, except in the discharge of their official functions.

Conflicts of Interest. Interpreters shall disclose any real or perceived conflict of interest, including any prior involvement with the case, parties, witnesses or attorneys, and shall not serve in any matter in which they have a conflict of interest.

Remuneration and Gifts. Court interpreters shall accept remuneration for their service to the court only from the court. Court interpreters shall not accept any gifts, gratuities, or valuable consideration from any litigant, witness, or attorney in a case in which the interpreter is serving the court, provided, however, that when no other court interpreters are available, the court may authorize court interpreters working for the court to provide interpreting services to, and receive compensation for such services from, an attorney in the case.

---

[10] *Standards for Performance and Professional Responsibility*, ADMIN. OFFICE OF THE U.S. COURTS, http://www.uscourts.gov/uscourts/FederalCourts/Interpreter/Standards_for_Performance.pdf.

4: Professional Demeanor

In the course of their service to the court, interpreters shall conduct themselves in a manner consistent with the dignity of the court and shall be as unobtrusive as possible.

5: Confidentiality

Interpreters shall protect the confidentiality of all privileged and other confidential information.

6: Restriction of Public Comment

Interpreters shall not publicly discuss, report, or offer an opinion concerning a matter in which they are or have been engaged, even when that information is not privileged or required by law to be confidential.

7: Scope of Practice

Interpreters shall limit themselves to interpreting or translating, and shall not give legal advice, express personal opinions to individuals for whom they are interpreting, or engage in any other activities which may be construed to constitute a service other than interpreting or translating while serving as an interpreter.

8: Assessing and Reporting Impediments to Performance

Interpreters shall assess at all times their ability to deliver their services. When interpreters have any reservation about their ability to satisfy an assignment competently, they shall immediately convey that reservation to the appropriate judicial authority.

9: Duty to Report Ethical Violations

Interpreters shall report to the proper judicial authority any effort to impede their compliance with any law, any provision of these Standards, or any other official policy governing court interpreting and legal translating.

APPENDIX 4: COURT INTERPRETER CERTIFICATION

I.   Languages for which certification is currently offered by the Administrative Office (AO)

    A.   Spanish

II.   Languages for which AO Certified Interpreters exist

    A.   Haitian Creole
    B.   Navajo
    C.   Spanish

The Court Interpreters Act of 1978 and the subsequent Amendments of 1988 (28 U.S.C. §§ 1827-1828) require the Director of the AO to define criteria for certifying interpreters qualified to interpret in federal courts. The Act also requires the Director to maintain a list of interpreters who have been certified. Certified interpreters are placed on an eligibility list from which court interpreters may be selected by the local officials of the United States District Courts. One important impact of the 1978 federal law was the creation and implementation of the Spanish/English Federal Court Interpreter Certification Examination (FCICE) in 1980.

The FCICE introduced to the court interpreting environment the concept of performance-based interpreter testing, which is based on rigorous testing practices. The requirements for passing the examination and for becoming a Federally Certified Court Interpreter (FCCI) reflect the knowledge, skills, and abilities required for court interpreting and the difficulty of the work. Although in the past the FCICE was offered for Spanish/English, Navajo/English, and Haitian Creole/English, it is now offered only for Spanish/English, since that is the primary interpreting need in the federal judiciary.

The FCICE is a two-phase examination of language proficiency and interpretation performance, consisting of a Written Examination and an Oral Examination. The two examinations are administered in alternate years. The first phase of the examination, referred to as the Written Examination, is a multiple-choice test of language proficiency in English and Spanish, and is offered in even-numbered years. The second phase is an Oral Examination that simulates the work that interpreters do in court, and is offered in odd-numbered years.

Candidates must pass the Phase One Written Examination to be eligible to take the Phase Two Oral Examination. Candidates who pass the Oral Examination will receive a letter and certificate from the Director of the AO awarding certification as a Federally Certified Court Interpreter (FCCI). The passing score is 75 percent for the Written Examination and 80 percent for the Oral Examination.

The examination is administered under the supervision of the AO, which contracts with specialists in court interpretation and language testing for development and administration of the examination.

APPENDIX 5: THE TELEPHONE INTERPRETING PROGRAM (TIP)

Introduction

The Administrative Office of the United States Courts (AO) has established the Judiciary's Telephone Interpreting Program (TIP) to provide remote interpretation for court proceedings where certified or highly qualified court interpreters are not reasonably available locally. In 1994, the Judicial Conference approved the program to provide simultaneous interpreting for short court proceedings. Some examples of short hearings are those that typically last 60 minutes or less, such as:

- Pretrial hearings;
- Initial appearances;
- Arraignments; and
- Probation and pretrial services interviews.

Most telephone interpreting through TIP is handled by staff interpreters at the provider courts. The provider courts contract with certified or otherwise-qualified interpreters for additional support as needed. All TIP services for events requiring Spanish are provided by federally certified court interpreters.

Benefits

The Judiciary's TIP provides many benefits, including:

- Ensures defendants in court proceedings initiated by the United States receive quality interpreting services from certified and highly qualified interpreters.

- Provides easy access to interpretation services when resources are not available locally.

- Increases court personnel efficiency in locating certified or otherwise qualified interpreters for scheduled court proceedings. Provider courts locate, contract with, conduct security checks on, and pay contract court interpreters providing TIP services.

- Reduces expenditures because staff and contract interpreters can be used for multiple assignments on the same day.

- Reduces time and travel cost associated with importing certified and otherwise qualified interpreters from outside the area.

Provider Courts

Only courts with staff interpreters can provide TIP services. Staffed courts can volunteer to become TIP providers and are free to choose to handle as many or few matters as their local schedules allow.

Participation in TIP

Equipment
A courtroom must be equipped with a two-line telephone system as well as some special equipment to receive simultaneous telephone interpreting services. The AO will provide funding for such equipment in districts that wish to receive TIP services. Courtrooms that have received technology upgrades may already have the necessary equipment. Should courts wish to become providers of TIP services, the AO will provide funding for provider-end equipment and training of a staff interpreter.

Access to TIP
The TIP scheduling system is available on the J-Net by selecting "Schedule an Interpreter" from the main TIP page. A step-by-step User's Guide is available from the TIP scheduling system home page. User courts may contact the TIP Help Desk at 571-535-0576 to request a login and to create a profile.

TIP Services by Contract Court Interpreters
Sometimes TIP services are requested in languages other than Spanish. When this happens, it is an opportunity for a provider court from a region with many language resources to assist courts in areas with fewer resources. The provider court can contract with a contract court interpreter to cover the event in the language needed. The first time that a new contract court interpreter covers a TIP event, experienced staff from the provider court will provide orientation on the use of the TIP equipment and remain with them until they are up to speed on its operation.

APPENDIX 6: COURTROOM LAYOUT

Although the exact layout of a federal courtroom can vary slightly from location to location, the same general features and components are present in courtrooms nationally.

Upon entering the first set of double doors on the way into a courtroom, there will usually be two rooms, one located on each side of the vestibule. These are the attorney/client and government/witness waiting rooms. Defense attorneys use the waiting rooms for private conferences with their investigators, out-of-custody clients or the defendant's family members. The Government uses the waiting rooms for their agents and officers and for victims and their advocates before and after hearings.

Through the next set of doors is the entrance to the courtroom itself. Immediately on the left and right, and often continuing for several rows is the public gallery, with seating for the general public on either side. Unless otherwise indicated, usually by a sign and/or locked doors, all court hearings are open to the public.

Continuing forward, there will be a railing with a set of small swinging doors, separating the public gallery from the well of the courtroom. Only authorized personnel are permitted to enter the well. The well of the courtroom is where the proceedings take place. The United States Marshal Service assists with court security and transports defendants that are detained. There are usually two Deputy United States Marshals in the courtroom when a defendant is in custody.

Once the location of the jury box has been identified, usually along an outside wall of the well, it will be easy to determine the role and location of participants present in the courtroom. The table located closest to the jury box is the Government's counsel table, usually occupied by an Assistant U.S. Attorney and sometimes an agent, depending on the hearing type. The counsel table on the opposite side is for the defense attorney and their client. The defense attorney can be either an Assistant Federal Public Defender, a Criminal Justice Act (CJA) panel attorney, or privately retained counsel.

In the middle of the well, between the counsel tables and the judge, there will usually be a lectern from which the attorneys present their arguments. In shorter proceedings such as initial appearances, the lectern is where the defendant and defense attorney stand during the event. If an interpreter is present, he or she will also stand at the lectern.

The judge sits at the bench in the very front of the courtroom. The witness stand is located on the judge's side that is closest to the jury box. The Courtroom Deputy Clerk (CD) and the Court Reporter sit lower down at the front of the courtroom, often on the opposite side of the judge from the jury box. The CD administers oaths to witnesses, marks exhibits, and helps proceedings run smoothly. The Court Reporter keeps the official record of the court proceeding using a stenographic machine.

Depending on the courthouse or hearing type, the interpreter may need to stand or sit in one of several locations in the court room.

Federal District Judge Courtrooms

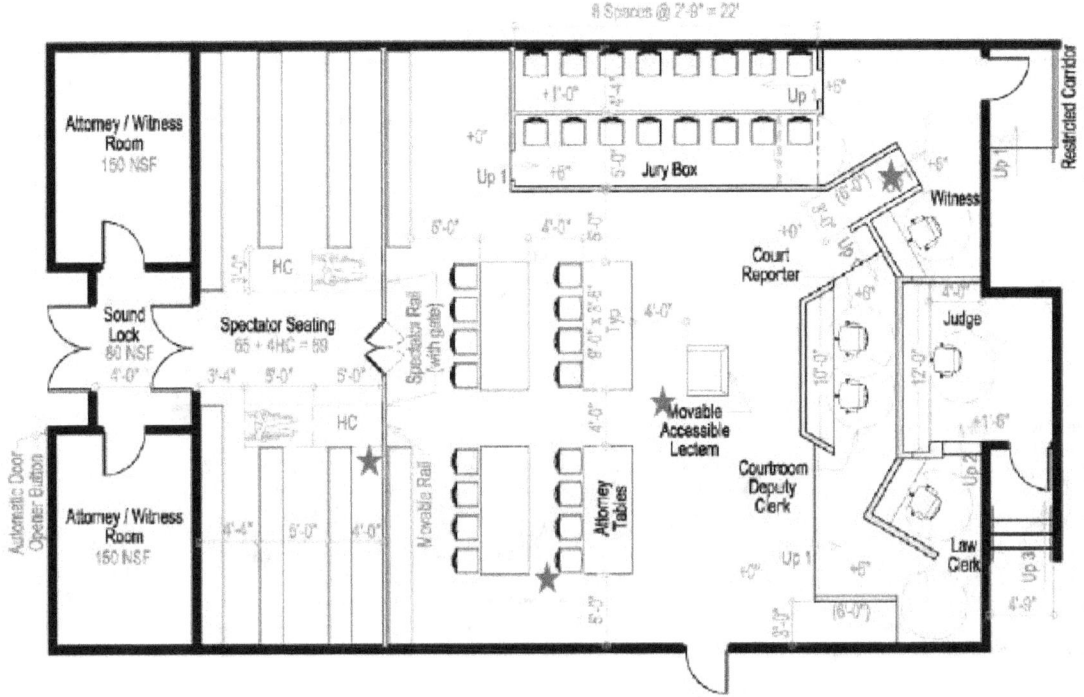

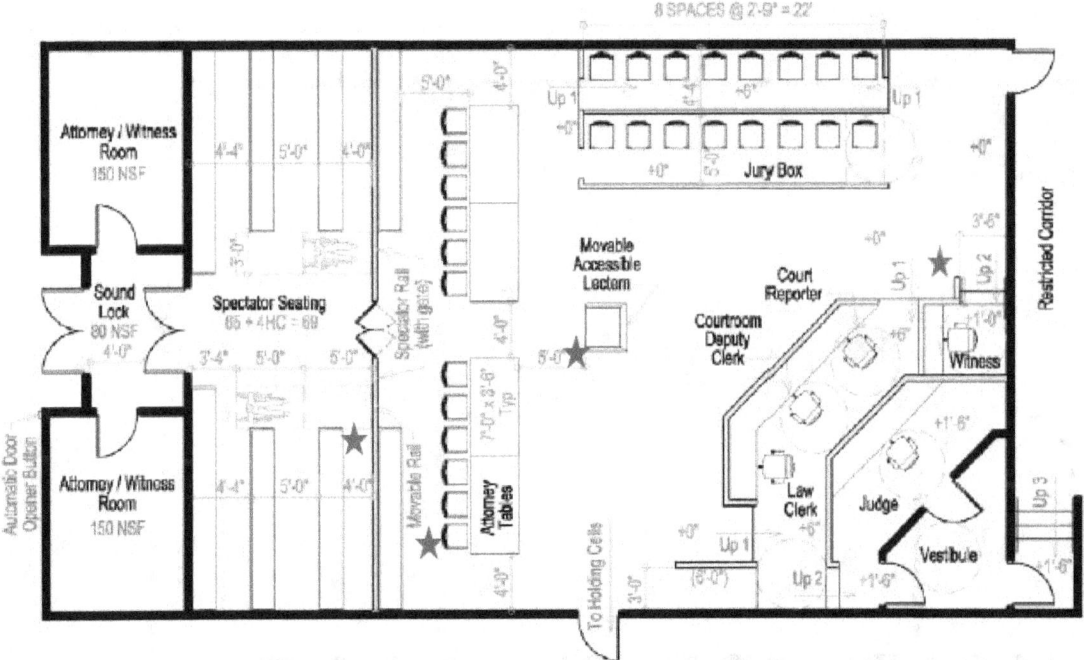

★ Indicates a possible interpreter location in the courtroom.

Federal Magistrate Judge Courtrooms

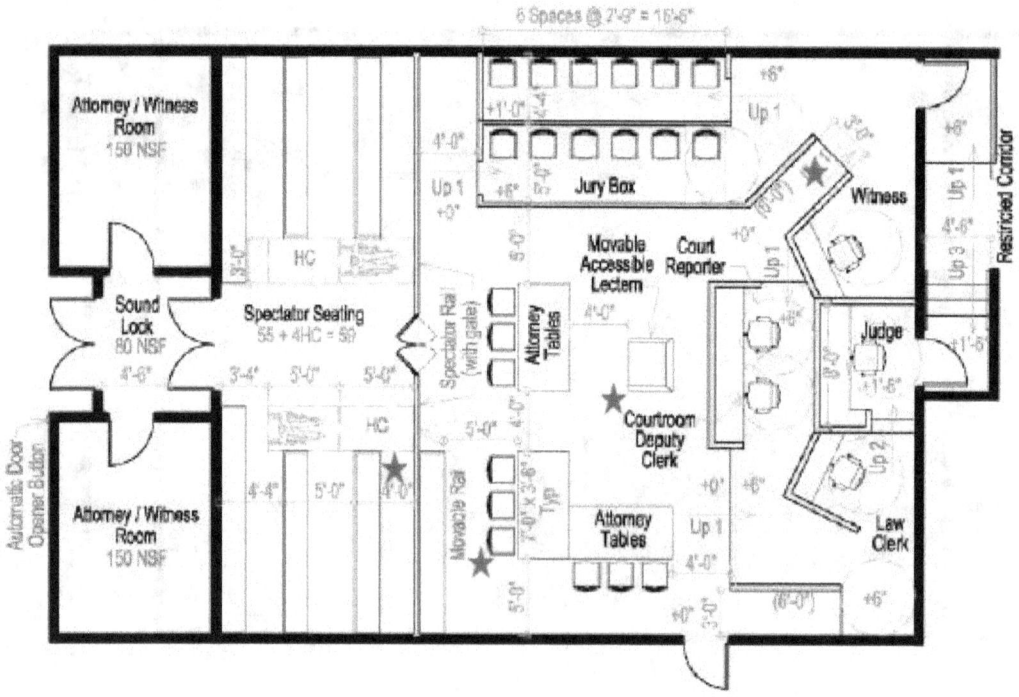

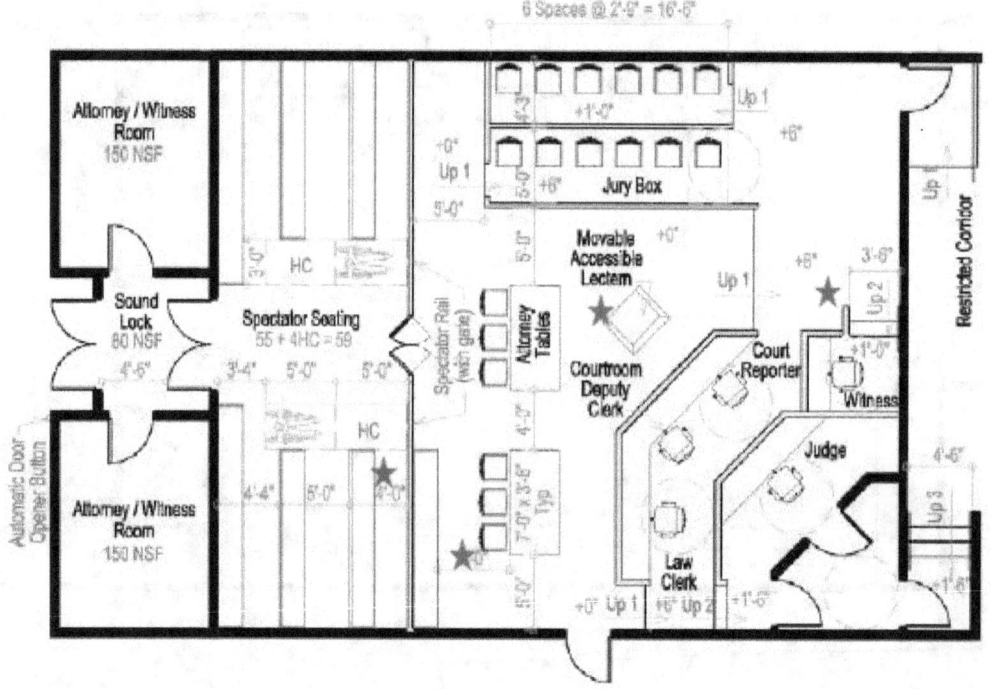

★ Indicates a possible interpreter location in the courtroom.

GLOSSARY

This Glossary has been compiled from a variety of sources to aid in understanding of the federal court system, the interpreting function, and general legal terminology[11,12]. Interpreters should be able to understand and identify all terminology presented in both the source and target languages.

Accuracy	The condition or quality of being true, correct, or exact; freedom from error or defect; precision or exactness; correctness.
Acquittal	A finding that the defendant is not guilty of the charges brought by the government. This finding may be reached by the trial judge in a case tried before a judge alone or by the jury in a case tried before a jury.
Administrative Office of the U.S. Courts	AOUSC or AO; the central support entity for the Judicial Branch. It provides a wide range of administrative, legal, financial, management, program, and information technology services to the federal courts. The AO provides support and staff counsel to the Judicial Conference of the United States and its committees, and implements and executes Judicial Conference policies, as well as applicable federal statutes and regulations.
Admissible	A term used to describe evidence that may be considered by a jury or judge in civil and criminal cases.
Admit/Deny Hearing	A hearing at which the statutory grounds set forth in the petition are admitted or denied.
Adversary System	A term often applied to the Anglo-American system for resolving criminal cases because that system involves pitting two adversaries, the government and the defendant, against each other in court. The underlying theory of the adversary system is that the clash between two equally matched adversaries is likely to yield the truth in a given case, that is, what actually happened.
Affidavit	A sworn written statement. Complaints, search warrants, and arrest warrants must be supported by affidavits establishing probable cause.
Allocution	An oral pleading or argument made to the court at sentencing by counsel for the defendant, the defendant, and the prosecutor. During allocution, the speaker attempts to persuade the judge that a particular sentence should or should not be imposed.
Appeal	A request made after a trial by a party that has lost on one or more issues that a higher court review the decision to determine if it was correct. To make such a request is "to appeal" or "to take an appeal." The party who appeals is called the "appellant;" and the other party is the "appellee." A defendant who has been found guilty after a trial has the right to appeal the conviction to the appropriate U.S. court of appeals and seek a new trial or other relief. Similarly, when authorized by statute, a party

---

[11] *How Criminal Cases Move Through District Courts, Glossary,* JNET, http://jnet.ao.dcn/District/Court_Reporting/Policy_and_Guidance/Federal_Court_System_Overview/How_Criminal _Cases_Move_Through_The_District_Courts/Glossary html

[12] *Glossary*, U.S. COURTS, http://www.uscourts.gov/Common/Glossary.aspx.

	adversely affected by a sentence imposed by the court or by a pretrial ruling of the court may appeal that sentence or ruling to the court of appeals and seek a different result.
Appointed Counsel	An attorney appointed by the court to represent a person, usually an indigent person.
Arraignment	When the defendant is brought before the court, informed of the charges, and called upon to enter a plea to the charges. The defendant is given a copy of the indictment or information before being called upon to enter a plea. This is the initial appearance of a criminal defendant (unless the matter has been continued from an earlier time).
Arrest	Occurs when, either through show of force or actual physical seizure, a law enforcement officer detains a person or otherwise leads that person to reasonably believe that he or she is not free to leave.
Assistant Federal Public Defender	The public defender fulfills the United States Constitution's Sixth Amendment right to counsel by representing those charged with a crime who cannot afford an attorney. The assistant federal public defender provides legal representation to clients charged with federal criminal offenses or involved in other matters mandated by the Act; meets with clients to establish meaningful attorney-client relationships; directs the defense investigation of alleged crimes or offenses; researches case law; prepares pretrial motions; reviews material received from the government as pretrial discovery; engages in plea negotiations; determines trial strategies and defense approaches that affect jury selection, opening statements and closing arguments, client testimony, and cross-examination of witnesses; conducts sentencing investigations and prepares sentencing memoranda, and represents clients at sentencing hearings; prepares post-trial motions; and represents clients at trial, on appeal, and in other courtroom proceedings.
Assistant United States Attorney	AUSA; A federal prosecutor who assists the U.S. Attorney in the judicial district by advocating the government's position in criminal cases before the court.
Bail Bond	The money or funds paid to secure the release of a person who has been charged with a crime for a future appearance in court; written guaranty or pledge which is purchased from a bonding company (usually an insurance firm) or by an individual (called a "bondsman") as security to guarantee some form of performance, including appearing for court hearings.
Bail/Bond Hearing	A judicial proceeding where the court determines if a person charged with a criminal offense should be released on bail and trusted to make any and all required court appearances up to and including a trial. If the court determines that there is no reason to believe the defendant will fail to show up for court appearances and that the accused is not likely to re-offend while on bail, it must release the defendant subject to whatever terms and conditions are deemed appropriate under the circumstances. Those conditions can require a defendant to maintain a specific address, report to the police, and not have contact with victims and witnesses. In

	addition, the court may require that one or more sureties pledge some assets or cash (via a bond) to act as assurance that the defendant will comply with the conditions of release.
Bench Trial	A trial before a judge without a jury. The judge decides questions of fact as well as questions of law.
Booking	The criminal justice system's process for creation of an administrative record of those arrested.
Burden of Proof	The duty to prove disputed facts. In civil cases, a plaintiff generally has the burden of proving his or her case. In criminal cases, the government has the burden of proving the defendant's guilt.
Case law	The law as established in previous court decisions. A synonym for legal precedent. Akin to common law, which springs from tradition and prior judicial decisions.
Certified Interpreter	An interpreter who has successfully passed all the required components of the Federal Court Interpreter Certification Examination administered under the auspices of the Administrative Office. All staff court interpreters must be federally certified court interpreters.
Challenge for Cause	A challenge to a proposed juror based on the contention that, as a matter of law, the juror cannot decide the case at hand fairly and impartially. A challenge for cause must be based on specific grounds. If granted, it has the effect of excusing the prospective juror from service on the jury.
Chambers	The offices of a judge and his or her staff.
Change of Plea	A guilty plea in a criminal case where the defendant had previously pled not guilty. It is referred to as a "change" because the defendant had pled "not guilty" to the charges during a previous proceeding, usually during the post indictment arraignment, and now has decided to plead guilty to the charges instead of going to trial.
Charges	A formal accusation made before a court by a prosecuting authority, usually in the form of a "charging document."
Civil Hearing	A hearing involving a dispute between individuals and/or organizations. The facts of the dispute could involve a contract, a lease, a physical injury experienced by an individual, a divorce, or many other issues. Nonetheless, all disputes or unresolved conflicts between individuals ultimately may be solved through civil litigation. Generally, the result desired by the person filing the lawsuit is to be compensated for damages. An alternative result is to have the court order another person to begin or stop some activity.
CJA 21 form	A court form for Authorization and Voucher for Expert and Other Services for payment requests under the Criminal Justice Act.
Clerk	The court officer who oversees administrative functions, especially managing the flow of cases through the court. With respect to the Court Interpreters Act, this is the clerk of the district court or the bankruptcy court or a court unit executive designated by the chief judge of the district court to implement the Act.
Closing Argument	The part of the trial at which each party summarizes the evidence and attempts to convince the judge or jury that the evidence supports its side

	of the case.
Colloquialism	A word or phrase that is not formal or literary, typically one used in ordinary or familiar conversation.
Common Law	The legal system that originated in England and is now in use in the United States, which relies on the articulation of legal principles in a historical succession of judicial decisions. Common law principles can be changed by legislation.
Community Defender	Although similar to a federal public defender, technically it is actually a nonprofit corporation that receives federal grant money and acts more independently from the federal judiciary. Community defenders engage in traditional legal representation along with social service support, policymaking and lobbying efforts, and community education or other outreach efforts.
Complaint (Civil)	The initial pleading that starts a civil action and states the basis for the court's jurisdiction, the basis for the plaintiff's claim, and the demand for relief. In some states, this pleading is called a petition.
Complaint (Criminal)	A written statement of the essential facts of the offense charged, made upon oath before a magistrate judge.
Conference Interpreter	An interpreter who works in multilingual meetings and renders a message from one language into another, naturally and fluently. Unlike court interpreters, conference interpreters adopt the delivery, tone and convictions of the speaker and often make necessary adjustments to the speech.
<u>Consecutive Interpretation</u>	The mode of interpretation used to interpret testimony given by a limited English proficiency (LEP) individual on the witness stand, or other statements for the record involving questions and answers, as well as for situations in which dialogue with the LEP individual develops, such as interviews. The interpreter verbally conveys the original message into the target language after the speaker has paused. Note taking is an essential tool for optimal performance during <u>consecutive interpreting</u>.
Contract Interpreter	An interpreter who is not an employee of the court, but is an independent contractor used for short durations to provide interpreting services. Contract court interpreters may be AO certified or otherwise qualified interpreters.
Counsel Table	The long table in front of the judge's bench where the parties and lawyers sit during the hearing or trial. The prosecution, or plaintiffs' attorney in a civil case, is always seated closest to the jury box.
Count	An allegation in an indictment or information, charging a defendant with a crime. An indictment may contain allegations that the defendant has committed more than one crime. Each allegation must be listed separately. The separate allegations are referred to as the counts of the indictment.
Court	A government entity authorized to resolve legal disputes. Lawyers often refer to the district or magistrate judge presiding over their case in the third person as "the court." For example, a lawyer may say, "The court sustained the objection," in describing a ruling made by a district or

	magistrate judge handling the case.
Court Interpreters Act	The Court Interpreters Act, 28 U.S.C. § 1827, provides that the Director of the Administrative Office of the United States Courts shall prescribe, determine, and certify the qualifications of persons who may serve as certified interpreters, when the Director considers certification of interpreters to be merited, for the hearing impaired (whether or not also speech impaired) and persons who speak only or primarily a language other than the English language, in judicial proceedings instituted by the United States.
Court Interpreters Advisory Group	CIAG; A group comprised of eight staff interpreters from a representative cross-section of district courts and any combination of three members who are clerks of court, district executives, chief deputy clerks, or court interpreter supervisors, which assists the AO in addressing current critical issues in and improvements to the court interpreting program.
Court Reporter	A person who makes a word-for-word record of what is said in court, generally by using a stenographic machine, shorthand or audio recording, and then produces a transcript of the proceedings upon request.
Criminal Justice Act	CJA; The Criminal Justice Act, 18 U.S.C. § 3006A, provides that all persons who are charged with federal criminal offenses and are financially unable to obtain a private attorney are entitled to appointment of counsel to represent them.
Cross Examination	The opportunity for the attorney (or an unrepresented party) to ask questions in court of a witness who has testified on behalf of the opposing party. Ordinarily, questions on cross-examination are designed to test the credibility of the witness or to emphasize facts that are favorable to the questioner's case.
Decorum	Dignified propriety of behavior, speech, dress, etc.
Deposition	An oral statement made before an officer authorized by law to administer oaths. Such statements are often taken to examine potential witnesses, to obtain discovery, or to be used later in trial.
Detention Hearing	In criminal law, a hearing to determine whether a defendant should be released pending trial. In family law, a hearing held by the juvenile court to determine whether a juvenile who is accused of delinquent conduct should be detained, continued in confinement, or released pending an adjudicatory hearing.
Dictionary	A book, optical disc, mobile device, or online lexical resource containing a selection of the words of a language, giving information about their meanings, pronunciations, etymologies, inflected forms, derived forms, etc., expressed in either the same or another language; lexicon; glossary.
Direct Examination	The initial questioning of a witness by the attorney who called that witness to the stand.
Director	The Director of the Administrative Office of the U.S. Courts or the Director's designee.
Direct Speech	The reporting of speech by repeating the actual words of a speaker. Also known as direct voice.

Discourse	Any unit of connected speech or writing longer than a sentence.
Dismissal	Termination of an action or claim without further hearing. In criminal cases, the act of voluntarily terminating a criminal prosecution by the prosecutor or judge. In civil cases, the act of terminating a lawsuit or one of its causes of action by the party who brought the claim or by the judge.
Disposition	The court's final determination of a lawsuit or criminal charge.
District Court	In the federal court system, a trial court for federal cases in a court district, which is all or a portion of a state. It can be a local court in some states.
District Judge	A public official, appointed by the President with the advice and consent of Congress, to hear and decide legal matters in a federal district court.
Docket	A log containing the complete history of each case in the form of brief chronological entries summarizing the court proceedings.
Evidence	Information presented in testimony or in documents which is used to persuade the fact finder (judge or jury) to decide the case in favor of one party or the other.
Evidentiary Hearing	A hearing held in open court before a district or magistrate judge at which the testimony of witnesses is taken and exhibits may be introduced into evidence, as opposed to a hearing at which only legal argument is presented.
Exhibit	A piece of physical evidence which is then marked for identification and/or introduced into evidence.
Extradition Hearing	A hearing to determine whether a person wanted by the requesting jurisdiction can be forced to return to the requestor jurisdiction to stand trial.
Fairness Hearing	A court hearing wherein the "fairness" of a proposed settlement is evaluated by the court and any objections to a proposed settlement are heard by the court.
Federally Certified Court Interpreter	FCCI; A court interpreter who has successfully passed both the written and oral portions of the Federal Court Interpreter Certification Examination in Spanish, Navajo, or Haitian Creole and who has received certification from the Director of the AO.
Federal Public Defender	FPD; An attorney employed by the federal courts on a full-time basis to provide legal defense to defendants who are unable to afford counsel. The judiciary administers the Federal Defender Program pursuant to the Criminal Justice Act.
Felony	A criminal offense for which the possible penalty exceeds one year in prison.
Gestures	A movement or position of the hand, arm, body, head, or face that is expressive of an idea, opinion, emotion, etc.
Glossary	A list of terms in a special subject, field, or area of usage, with accompanying definitions.
Government	The sovereign power in a nation or state.
Grand Jury	A jury in each federal court district which serves for a term of a year and is composed of a group of citizens empaneled by the court to hear evidence and determine whether there is probable cause to return an

	indictment against a defendant. The Federal Rules of Criminal Procedure require that 16 to 23 persons sit on a grand jury.
Guilty	Having been convicted of a crime or civil wrongdoing or having admitted the commission of a crime or civil wrongdoing by pleading "guilty" (saying you did it).
Guilty plea	In criminal law, an accused person's formal admission in court of having committed the charged offense. A guilty plea must be made voluntarily and only after the accused has been informed of and understands his or her rights. It ordinarily has the same effect as a guilty verdict and conviction after a trial on the merits.
Hearing	A proceeding before a district or magistrate judge, without a jury, in which evidence and/or argument is presented to determine some issue of fact and/or law.
Hedging	To make advance arrangements to safeguard oneself from loss of an investment, speculation or bet, as when a buyer of commodities insures against unfavorable price changes by buying in advance at a fixed rate for later delivery.
Hung Jury	A jury which is unable to reach a unanimous agreement on a verdict in a criminal case.
Idiomatic Expression	An expression which has a figurative meaning.
Impaneling of the Jury	The act of selecting a jury from the list of potential jurors, called the "panel" or "venire."
Indictment	The formal charge issued by a grand jury stating that there is enough evidence that the defendant committed the crime to justify having a trial; it is used primarily for felonies
Information	A formal accusation by a government attorney that the defendant committed a misdemeanor.
Initial Appearance	A proceeding at which the magistrate judge informs the defendant of the nature of the charges. The defendant is also informed of the right to counsel, the right to remain silent, and the right to have a preliminary examination. After informing the defendant of these rights, the magistrate judge decides whether to release or detain the defendant. The Federal Rules of Criminal Procedure require that following an arrest, the defendant be taken before the nearest available magistrate judge without unnecessary delay.
Innocent	Freedom from legal or specific wrong; guiltlessness. In our criminal justice system, a defendant is considered innocent until proven guilty. Interpreters should be careful not to conflate a plea or verdict of "not guilty" with being a plea or verdict of innocence.
Interpretation	The oral rendering of the full and accurate meaning of speech from one language into another.
Interrogatories	A form of discovery consisting of written questions to be answered in writing and under oath.
Joinder	The joining together of two or more offenses, or two or more defendants, in the same indictment for purposes of trial.

Judge	An official of the Judicial Branch with authority to decide lawsuits brought before courts. Used generically, the term judge may also refer to all judicial officers, including Supreme Court justices.
Judgment	The official decision of a court finally resolving the dispute between parties to the lawsuit.
Judge or Presiding Judicial Officer	A U.S. district judge, bankruptcy judge, or magistrate judge.
Judicial Conference of the United States	The policy-making entity for the federal court system. A 27-judge body whose presiding officer is the Chief Justice of the United States.
Jurisdiction	The legal authority of a court to hear and decide a certain type of case. It also is used as a synonym for venue, meaning the geographic area over which the court has territorial jurisdiction to decide cases.
Jury	The group of persons selected to hear the evidence in a trial and render a verdict on matters of fact. In a criminal trial, there are 12 jurors plus alternates. The jury's duty is to weigh the evidence fairly and impartially and then decide whether the defendant is guilty or not guilty.
Jury Instructions	Directives given by a judge to a jury during a trial prescribing the manner in which the jurors should proceed in deciding the case at bar and providing guidance on the relevant law.
Jury Poll	The practice of affirming the assent of each jury member individually. After a jury verdict is returned but before it is officially recorded, the jury may be polled at the request of either party, usually the defense. During the poll, each juror is asked whether he or she agrees with the verdict announced by the foreperson.
Jury Selection	The process by which the adversaries select a jury. The prosecutor and the defense attorney jointly select the jury by using challenges to eliminate those jurors that they believe are biased or unsympathetic to their respective case.
Jury Trial	A trial of a lawsuit or criminal prosecution in which the case is presented to a jury and the factual questions and the final judgment are determined by a jury.
Language of Limited Diffusion	LLD; A language used in a country by a group which is significantly smaller in number than the rest of the population, also called a linguistic or language minority. Those who speak the language may be nationals of the country, but they have distinguishing ethnic, religious, or cultural features which they wish to safeguard.
Languages other than Spanish	LOTS; All languages other than the Spanish language. Sometimes referred to as OTS.
Leading Question	A question which, by its phrasing, suggests to the witness the answer desired by counsel. For example, the phrasing of the question, "The car was blue, wasn't it?" suggests that the questioner wants the witness to testify that the car was blue. Leading questions are allowed on cross-examination but not on direct examination.
Limited English Proficiency Person	LEP; Individuals who speak only or primarily a language other than the English language. Sometimes referred to as a limited English proficient individual.

Local Rules	A particular set of rules for each court governing matters not determined by the Federal Rules of Procedure. Each U.S. district court is authorized to "make and amend rules governing its practice not inconsistent with" the Federal Rules of Procedure.
Lock-up	The area in a courthouse where detained defendants in a criminal matter are held until a hearing is called. Security for the lock-up is under the jurisdiction of the U.S. Marshal.
Magistrate judge	A judicial officer of a federal district court, who conducts initial proceedings in criminal cases, decides criminal misdemeanor cases, conducts many pretrial civil and criminal matters on behalf of district judges, and decides civil cases with the consent of the parties.
Misdemeanor	A criminal offense that is less serious than a felony and for which the maximum penalty is one year in prison.
Mistrial	A ruling by the court that the trial is to be terminated and given no effect because of an error in the proceedings. The court may also declare a mistrial when the jury is unable to agree on a verdict. When a mistrial is declared, the trial must start again with the selection of a new jury.
Motion	A request by either the government (or plaintiff in a civil case) or the defense for a ruling by the court on a particular matter. Motions filed before trial are generally referred to as pretrial motions. All motions, other than those made during a trial or hearing must be in writing, unless the court permits them to be made orally.
Motion Hearing	A motion hearing is a proceeding in which each party has the opportunity to present his or her side of an issue of particular importance to a case in court.
Motion to Suppress	A motion (usually on behalf of a criminal defendant) to disallow certain evidence, alleged to have been seized illegally.
Nebbia Hearing	A hearing in which the court must decide whether or not the money or property posted as bail is the fruit of unlawful or criminal conduct.
Nolo Contendere	No contest. As far as the criminal sentence is concerned, a plea of nolo contendere has the same effect as a plea of guilty. However, this plea may not be considered as an admission of guilt for any other purpose.
Not guilty	1) plea of a person who claims not to have committed the crime of which he/she is accused, made in court when arraigned (first brought before a judge) or at a later time set by the court. 2) verdict after trial stating that the prosecution has not proved the defendant guilty of a crime beyond a reasonable doubt or that the defendant was insane at the time the crime was committed.
Note-taking	The practice of writing down pieces of information in a systematic way.
Objection	When an attorney alerts the judge to potential problems which may be caused by admission of evidence. An attorney who disagrees with a ruling by the court must register an objection to that ruling in order to make the trial record clear and establish the right to object to the ruling before the appellate court, should there be an appeal.
Opening statement	The initial address to the jury that the attorneys for each side make after the jury is sworn to explain what evidence they intend to present during

	the course of the trial and what they believe that evidence will show.
Opinion	A judge's written explanation of the decision of the court.
Oral Argument	An opportunity for lawyers to summarize their position before the court and also to answer the judges' questions.
Otherwise Qualified Interpreter	An interpreter, not certified by the AO, who can competently interpret in court proceedings. Interpreters who meet specific AO standards described in §320.20 of Volume 5 of the *Guide to Judiciary Policy* may be deemed "professionally qualified."
Overrule	The ruling of the court when there is no merit to an objection made to a question asked of a witness. The witness is then allowed to answer the question.
Panel attorney	A private attorney who represents an indigent defendant at the government's expense. A panel attorney is usually a member of an affiliated list and assigned by a court to a particular case.
Peremptory Challenge	A challenge to a prospective juror for which no specific reason need be given. A successful peremptory challenge has the effect of excusing the prospective juror from service on a particular jury. The number of peremptory challenges available to the government and the defense varies, depending on whether the case is a capital felony, felony, or misdemeanor.
Petit jury	A jury (usually consisting of 6 or 12 persons) summoned and impaneled in the trial of a specific case.
Plea	In a criminal case, the defendant's statement pleading "guilty" or "not guilty" in answer to the charges.
Plea Agreement	An agreement between the government and the defendant to resolve a pending criminal case by the defendant's entry of a guilty plea rather than going to trial. The prosecutor may agree to dismiss or reduce certain charges, or to recommend or request a certain sentence in return for the defendant's entering a plea of guilty.
Plea Hearing	A hearing scheduled for the entry of a plea, usually a guilty plea associated with a plea bargain.
Preliminary Hearing	A hearing to determine if a person charged with a felony should be tried for the crime charged, based on whether there is sufficient evidence that he/she committed the crime. Sometimes referred to as a preliminary examination.
Presentence Investigation and/or Report	An inquiry into the defendant's background, financial condition, criminal offense(s), and criminal history performed by the probation officer. The probation officer incorporates the information revealed by this investigation in a presentence report. The report is prepared to assist the judge in deciding how to sentence the defendant. The investigation is sometimes referred to informally as the PSI (presentence investigation) and the resulting document is often called the PSR (presentence report).
Pretrial Conference	Pretrial hearing; an informal meeting at which opposing attorneys confer to work toward the disposition of the case by discussing matters of evidence and narrowing the issues that will be tried.
Pretrial Proceedings	The events that occur between the time the defendant first appears in

	court and the time of trial. These events may include a detention hearing, a preliminary examination, an arraignment, discovery, and filing pretrial motions.
Pretrial Release	Occurs when a judge allows a criminal defendant pre-trial freedom, based on the past history of the defendant, roots in the community, regular employment, the recommendation of the AUSA, the type of crime, the likelihood of the defendant making all appearances in court, and the improbability that the defendant will commit another crime while awaiting trial.
Pretrial Services	Functions performed by a federal court before committing a person to trial. It involves screening services and investigation which may lead to community supervision that takes place after a person has been charged and arrested with a federal crime
Pretrial Services Interview	An initial interview of a defendant that assists the court in deciding whether a defendant will be released or kept in custody pending trial. The Pretrial Services Officer shall advise the defendant of the right to speak with a lawyer before answering questions, and shall further advise the defendant that if the defendant cannot afford a lawyer, one will be appointed.
Pretrial services officer	An officer who works with defendants prior to trial, but after they're charged with federal crimes. Pretrial services officers help ensure that defendants released to the community before trial commit no crime while awaiting trial and return to court as required.
Probable cause	Sufficient reason based upon known facts to believe a crime has been committed or that certain property is connected with a crime; more than a bare suspicion.
Probation	A court-imposed criminal sentence that, subject to stated conditions, releases a convicted person into the community instead of sending the criminal to jail or prison.
Probation Officer	An officer who is responsible for conducting presentence investigations and preparing presentence reports prior to sentencing and for supervising probationers and persons on supervised release. Probation officers also serve as parole officers for offenders released by the United States Parole Commission, that is, offenders sentenced for offenses committed before November 1, 1987.
Prosecute	To charge someone with a crime. An AUSA tries a criminal case on behalf of the government.
Public defender	A staff lawyer, usually publicly appointed, whose duty is to represent indigent criminal defendants.
Re-arraignment	The process of arraignment of a defendant after amendment of the accusatory pleading or the substitution of an indictment or information for another.
Reasonable doubt	The doubt that prevents one from being firmly convinced of a defendant's guilt, or the belief that there is a real possibility that a defendant is not guilty.
Record	A written account of the proceedings in a case, including all pleadings,

	evidence, and exhibits submitted in the course of the case.
Regionalisms	A feature, such as an expression, a pronunciation, or a custom that is characteristic of a geographic area.
Relay Interpretation	A type of interpretation that occurs when no interpreter is available to interpret a language of limited diffusion (LLD) into English, but one can interpret the needed language into another language for which there is an available, qualified interpreter. The non-English speaking interpreter "relays" the interpretation into the common language and the second interpreter relays this into English and vice versa. (Examples: Mixteco to Spanish to English or Tactile Signing to American Sign Language (ASL) to English.) *Guide to Judiciary Policy*, Vol. 5, Ch. 1, §140.
Rendition	Translation; interpretation.
Retained counsel	Legal counsel who are members of the bar working in the private sector, either individually or in law firms, who are hired to provide legal services, generally for a fee.
Reverse	The act of a court setting aside the decision of a lower court. A reversal is often accompanied by a remand to the lower court for further proceedings.
Revocation of probation or supervised release	An offender who violates one or more conditions of probation runs the risk that the sentence of probation may be revoked. Upon revocation, the offender may be sentenced to a term of imprisonment. The same is true for persons on supervised release.
Sentence	A judgment of the court imposing punishment upon a defendant for criminal conduct.
Sentencing Hearing	The hearing that takes place after the defendant is found guilty of a crime. The purpose of a sentencing hearing is to determine what punishment the defendant deserves for the crime he/she committed. At the hearing, the court considers the attorneys' comments on the probation officer's recommendations, allows the attorneys to state their positions regarding sentencing, and gives the defendant an opportunity to make a statement.
Settlement Hearing	A settlement hearing is a hearing in which both parties try to reach an agreement on what will be paid or charged regarding an offense or civil judgment.
Sight Translation	Conveying orally in one language the meaning of a text written in another language. It is a hybrid of translation and interpretation that requires the interpreter to first review the original written text, and then render it orally into the other language.
Simultaneous Interpretation	The full and accurate rendering of speech from one language into another while the speaker or signer is still talking. This requires the interpreter to listen, comprehend, translate, and reproduce a speaker or signer's message while the speaker or signer continues to speak or sign, typically lagging a matter of seconds behind the speaker or signer's communication. The simultaneous mode is used by interpreters when interpreting all that is said in courtroom proceedings for non-English speaking defendants or other participants as defined in the Guide, Vol 5 §

	<u>210.10 and § 255.20(c).</u>
Simultaneous Interpretation Equipment	Electronic equipment that allows the interpreter to interpret into a microphone and the interpreted speech to be sent in real time via a transmitter to a receiver (earphones) for one or more defendants. The use of such equipment also enables interpreters to better position themselves where they can hear and see the speakers without strain and to serve multiple defendants at the same time.
Source Language	The language from which a statement in another language is translated or interpreted.
Staff Interpreter	An employee of the court who has passed the necessary written and oral exams to be certified as Federally Certified Court Interpreter (FCCI)
Standard of Proof	Degree of proof required. In criminal cases, prosecutors must prove guilt "beyond a reasonable doubt." The majority of civil lawsuits require proof "by a preponderance of the evidence" (50 percent plus), but in some the standard is higher and requires "clear and convincing" proof.
Status Conference	A pre-trial meeting of attorneys before a judge required under Federal Rules of Civil Procedure and in many states required to inform the court as to how the case is proceeding, what discovery has been conducted (depositions, interrogatories, production of documents), any settlement negotiations, probable length of trial and other matters relevant to moving the case toward trial.
Status Hearing	An informal discussion between the judge, the prosecution and the defendant about the case. After considering the case, the defendant can decide whether to change his/her plea or to continue with trial.
Stipulation	An agreement between the defendant and the prosecutor. The stipulation may take the form of an agreed-upon term or condition in a legal document or an agreement between the parties establishing a certain fact as evidence during a trial. When a fact is stipulated to during a trial, no evidence of that fact is required because the parties have agreed to accept it as true.
Subpoena	A court order requiring a person to appear at a trial or hearing for the purpose of testifying as a witness. Under the Sixth Amendment, a criminal defendant has the right to compulsory process, that is, the right to subpoena witnesses to testify for the defense at trial. The government may also subpoena witnesses for trial. A subpoena may also order a witness to bring to a trial or hearing certain documents which are relevant to the case.
Substitution of Counsel	Occurs when an individual/party to a case wishes to change legal representation or substitute another attorney/law firm for the one currently handling the matter, and petitions the court to do so.
<u>**Summary Interpreting**</u>	The rendering of speech from one language into another while paraphrasing and condensing the speaker's statement. Unlike simultaneous and consecutive interpreting, summary interpreting <u>does not provide a full and accurate rendering</u> of everything that is said into the target language. Summary interpreting should not be used in the legal setting. For more information, visit to watch a short video.

Summons	A court order commanding an individual to appear before a magistrate judge at a certain time to answer charges. A summons is similar to an arrest warrant, except that a summons directs the defendant to appear on his own before a magistrate judge. An arrest warrant is a court order that he or she be arrested and be brought to the nearest available district or magistrate judge by a law enforcement officer.
Supervised Release	A term of supervision served after a person is released from prison. The court imposes supervised release during sentencing in addition to the sentence of imprisonment. Unlike parole, supervised release does not replace a portion of the sentence of imprisonment but is in addition to the time spent in prison. U.S. probation officers supervise people on supervised release.
Suppression Hearing	An opportunity to have a judge look at the evidence against a defendant and determine whether it will be allowed at trial. Generally, this is the time when opposing parties will present their arguments to a judge regarding a Motion to Suppress.
Sustain	The ruling of the court when it determines that the objection to a question asked of a witness has merit and that the questions must not be answered. For example, if the court sustains a prosecutor's objection to the form of a question posed by defense counsel, the witness is not allowed to answer the question until counsel phrases it properly.
Target Language	The language into which a statement in another language is translated or interpreted.
Team Interpreting	The use of two or more interpreters for trials or lengthy hearings. The interpreter not actively interpreting (known as the passive interpreter) researches terms, takes notes, monitors the interpretation being provided, Guide to Judiciary Policy, Vol. 5, Ch. 1, §140, and provides support to the active interpreter. Team interpreters alternate roles during the interpreted event. Also known as tandem interpreting.
Teamwork	A coordinated effort on the part of a group of persons acting together as a team or in the interests of a common cause.
Telephone Interpreting	A service that connects interpreters via telephone to individuals who need to communicate with each other but do not share a common language. Interpretation over the telephone most often takes place in consecutive mode, which means that the interpreter waits until the speaker finishes an utterance before rendering the interpretation into the target language.
Telephone Interpreting Program	TIP; A system which provides simultaneous and consecutive interpreting for short proceedings using specialized equipment. TIP provides remote interpreting in situations where on-site court interpreters are not available or cost-effective.
Testimony	Oral evidence given under oath by a witness in answer to questions posed by attorneys at trial or at a deposition (questioning under oath outside of court).
Transcription	The production of a written text that reflects an oral message as it is spoken. Both the original spoken message and the parallel written text

	are in the same language.
Transcription and Translation of Recordings	The reproduction in writing of the original spoken words recorded on tape or other media in a source language, and their subsequent translation into the target language as part of a transcript.
Translation	The transference of meaning of a written document from the source language into the target language in writing. The translator is given a text and prepares an accurate parallel text in writing, without the pressure of immediate delivery.
Transparency	Openness, clarity; lack of guile and attempts to hide damaging information. The word is used of financial disclosures, organizational policies and practices, lawmaking, and other activities where organizations interact with the public.
Trial	A formal judicial examination of evidence and determination of legal claims in an adversarial proceeding.
United States Attorney	A lawyer appointed by the President in each judicial district to prosecute and defend cases for the federal government. The U.S. Attorney employs a staff of Assistant U.S. Attorneys who appear as the government's attorneys in individual cases.
Unites States Marshals Service	The U.S. Marshals Service is the nation's enforcement arm of the federal courts, involved in virtually every federal law enforcement initiative. Presidentially appointed, U.S. marshals direct the activities of 94 districts — one for each federal judicial district. Among their many duties, they protect the federal judiciary, apprehend federal fugitives, seize property acquired by criminals through illegal activities, house and transport federal prisoners and operate the Witness Security Program.
Unobtrusive	Inconspicuous, unassertive, or reticent.
Uphold	The appellate court agrees with the lower court decision and allows it to stand.
Utterance	An oral or written statement; a stated or published expression
Verdict	The decision of a trial jury or a judge that determines the guilt or innocence of a criminal defendant, or that determines the final outcome of a civil case.
Voir dire	The jury selection process of questioning prospective jurors, to ascertain their qualifications and determine any basis for challenge. A voir dire process may also be used by the presiding judicial officer to question an interpreter on the record about their credentials and qualifications for the interpreting assignment.
Waiver	The act of knowingly, intentionally, and voluntarily giving up a certain right. For example, a defendant who intends to plead guilty must first waive his/her right to a jury trial in order for the guilty plea to be accepted by the court.
Warrant	Court authorization, most often for law enforcement officers, to conduct a search or make an arrest.
Witness	A person called upon by either side in a legal proceeding to give testimony before the court or jury.